The Ultimate Instant Pot Duo Crisp Air Fryer Cookbook

1000 Days Duo Crisp Air Fryer Recipes with Color Pictures
for Beginners and Advanced Users
(Full Color Edition)

Thomas Rosales

CONTENT

Introduction

Ever since I started cooking, I have used a lot of traditional methods – conventional cookers, pressure cookers and pretty much every form of cooking that I can think of. But over the last few years the thing that I have enjoyed cooking with most is the air fryer. I have used different brands of air fryers and I have discovered that each air fryer has its unique features. Each air fryer has specific recipes it works perfectly for. Thus, I always have my reservation when it comes to endorsing brands of air fryers.

What I do most times is to recommend certain brands of air fryers to people who come to me for advice. My recommendations are based on how much time they have to cook, the kind of foods they love to cook and the kind of recipes that they would love to try.

One of the brands of air fryers that I have found particularly useful for cooking my recipes is the Instant Pot Duo Crisp Air Fryer. I have used it over time and seen its capacity and usefulness. I will not only recommend it to you. I will also share important details you need to know about it.

Chapter 1: What is an Instant Pot Duo Crisp Air Fryer

The Instant Pot Duo Crisp Air Fryer is a stainless-steel pressure cooker and air fryer combo, with an 8-quart capacity. The unit is fairly heavy, weighing around 22 pounds and measuring around 15 inches long, 14 inches wide and around 15 inches high.

If you are looking for something to carry around, this air fryer is not what you need, and it might take some space in your kitchen. However, the air fryer more than compensates for it size by being able to cook food for 8 people. Also, its 11-in-1 functionality allows it to serve various roles. It can air fry, roast, bake, dehydrate, pressure cook, slow cook, cook rice, make yogurt, steam, serve as sauté pan, sterilize and warm food. What this means is that you will probably no longer need all your former cookers

In addition to its regular features, this cooker also comes with double lids, a pressure cooker Lid and an air fryer lid. The pot inside the air fryer is also made of stainless steel like the fryer's body. It comes with an air fryer basket, and a broiling tray.

Why the Instant Pot Duo Crisp Air Fryer is the best

The Instant Pot Duo Crisp Air fryer is based on the Evencrisp technology which is designed to make it deliver all the crunch and tenderness of deep-frying with only 5% of the oil usage of a conventional cooker.

With this cooker, you can enjoy a quick one-touch of button cooking control. It has 11 settings of a customizable Smart Programs to choose from. You can pressure cook and air fry ribs, soups, beans, rice, poultry, sea food yogurt, desserts and pretty much any kind of food you fancy. It is all the control I want over my cooking in one device

The air fryers inner cooking pot is extremely versatile. Its food-grade stainless-steel cooking pot with a tri-ply bottom offers you more options for cooking what you want. It also features an anti-spin design that secures the pot that helps me to make perfect sautéed foods.

As I have pointed out, you can cook fast with the pressure cooker or slow cook your favorite traditional recipes. This is one more reason to choose this fryer over a normal cooker because no cooker can give you that kind of control.

It is very easy to clean. Being made of stainless-steel means that both the external part of the Instant Pot Duo Crisp Air Fryer and the inner pot of the air fryer are finger-print resistant. This means you no longer to worry about your kids or any pets smudging it with dirty fingers or paws. All you need is just to wash it with mild soap and warm water and it will come out shiny and good as new.

How to clean up your Instant Pot Duo Crisp Air Fryer

The manual of the Instant Pot Duo Crisp Air Fryer says the unit is dishwasher compliant but in case you are like me and skeptical about putting it in your dishwasher, here are some cleaning methods that I usually recommend.

• Clean your fryer after every use, especially if you just used it to fry poultry or seafood. In that case it is preferable if you clean it before the inner pot becomes cold and the food debris sticks to it. However, don't clean it immediately after use, because it can cause burns.
• Clean the removable components of the air fryer with warm, soapy water. Use a soft sponge or cloth. If you must use detergents or soap at all make sure it is a mild detergent. Using an industrial cleaning agent might dull the steel's shine or scratch the inner pot.
• In case food is stuck on any of the parts of the air fryer, remove the parts and soak them in hot water and dish detergent to loosen the food, then clean as directed
• Clean the inside of the air fryer using a damp cloth dipped in warm soapy water.
• Wipe the exterior. Use a damp cloth or sponge, then dry the appliance.

So, there you have it. The Instant Pot Duo Crisp Air Fryer gives you everything you could ever want as an amateur or a professional cook and is guaranteed 100% satisfaction every time you use it. Hence, get those spoons, forks, nice and tongs and get ready to enjoy an amazing cooking experience.

Chapter 2: Basics

Roasted Vegetable Stock

Prep time: 10 minutes | Cook time: 1 hour 30 minutes | Serves 8

8 stalks celery, cut in half
4 medium sweet onions, peeled and quartered
4 medium carrots, cut in half
4 Roma tomatoes, cut in half
1 fennel bulb, quartered
1 medium green bell pepper, seeded and quartered

4 cloves garlic, peeled and crushed
2 tablespoons olive oil
5 sprigs fresh parsley
5 sprigs fresh tarragon
2 bay leaves

1. Preheat oven to 400ºF (204ºC). Place celery, onions, carrots, tomatoes, fennel, bell pepper, and garlic on a large rimmed baking sheet. Drizzle with oil and toss to coat. 2. Roast for 1 hour, turning vegetables every 10 minutes to avoid burning. If vegetables start to blacken, remove them from the baking sheet. 3. Add roasted vegetables, parsley, tarragon, and bay leaves to the pressure cooker, then fill pot with water to the Max Fill line. Close and lock the pressure cooker lid, set steam release to Sealing, select Pressure Cook and set time to 30 minutes at High pressure. Press Start. 4. When pressure cooking is complete, let pressure release naturally, about 30 minutes. Open lid. Strain stock into a jar and use immediately, refrigerate for up to seven days, or freeze for up to three months.

Herb Stock

Prep time: 5 minutes | Cook time: 15 minutes | Serves 4

4 cups water
3 bay leaves
2 cloves garlic, crushed
1 teaspoon whole black peppercorns

A handful of rosemary
2 sprigs parsley
½ teaspoon salt

1. Put all of the ingredients, except salt, into the pressure cooker. 2. Close and lock the pressure cooker lid. Select Pressure Cook and set time to 15 minutes at High pressure. Press Start. 3. When pressure cooking is complete, let the pressure release naturally for 10 minutes, and then release any remaining steam manually. Open the lid. 4. Season with salt to taste. 5. Strain the stock and pour into jars. Store in the refrigerator or freeze.

Mushroom Stock

Prep time: 10 minutes | Cook time: 30 minutes | Serves 8

1 tablespoon olive oil
1 medium yellow onion, unpeeled and chopped
2 stalks celery, chopped
4 cups sliced mushrooms
1 medium carrot, unpeeled and chopped

4 ounces (113 g) dried mixed mushrooms
3 cloves garlic, peeled and smashed
2 sprigs fresh thyme
2 bay leaves
1 tablespoon nutritional yeast

1. Press the Sauté button on the pressure cooker and heat oil. Add onion, celery, sliced mushrooms, and carrot. Cook, stirring often, for 5 minutes. Press the Cancel button. 2. Add dried mushrooms, garlic, thyme, bay leaves, and nutritional yeast to pot, then fill pot with water to the Max Fill line. Close and lock the pressure cooker lid, set steam release to Sealing, select Pressure Cook and set time to 30 minutes at High pressure. Press Start. 3. When pressure cooking is complete, let pressure release naturally, about 30 minutes. Open lid. Strain stock into a jar and use immediately, refrigerate for up to seven days, or freeze for up to three months.

Easy Jasmine Rice

Prep time: 2 minutes | Cook time: 4 minutes | Serves 4 to 6

2 cups jasmine rice
2 cups water

2 teaspoons olive oil
½ teaspoon salt

1. Rinse the rice well. 2. Transfer the rice to the pressure cooker. Add the water, oil and salt and stir. 3. Close and lock the pressure cooker lid. Select Pressure Cook and set time to 4 minutes at High pressure. Press Start. 4. When pressure cooking is complete, allow to naturally release for 10 minutes, then release the remaining pressure manually. Open the lid. 5. Fluff the rice with a fork and serve.

Madagascar Pink Rice

Prep time: 2 minutes | Cook time: 5 minutes | Serves 4 to 6

1 cups pink rice
1 cups water

½ teaspoon salt

1. Rinse the rice well. 2. Add the rice, water and salt to the pressure cooker, stir. 3. Close and lock the pressure cooker lid. Select Pressure Cook and set time to 5 minutes at High pressure. Press Start. 4. When pressure cooking is complete, let the pressure release naturally for 10 minutes, then release any remaining steam manually. Open the pot. 5. Fluff the rice with the rice spatula or fork. Serve.

Pork Broth

Prep time: 10 minutes | Cook time: 60 minutes | Serves 8

3 pounds (1.4 kg) pork bones
8 cups water
3 large carrots, cut into large chunks
3 large stalks celery, cut into large chunks

1 bay leaf
2 cloves garlic, sliced
1 tablespoon apple cider vinegar
1 teaspoon whole peppercorns
Salt, to taste

1. Dump all of the ingredients into the pressure cooker and give it a little stir to mix everything evenly. 2. Close and lock the pressure cooker lid. Select Pressure Cook and set time to 60 minutes at High pressure. Press Start. 3. When pressure cooking is complete, select Cancel and let naturally release for 10 minutes. Release any remaining steam manually. Uncover the pot. 4. Strain the broth and pour into jars. Store in the refrigerator or freeze.

Perfect Quinoa

Prep time: 2 minutes | Cook time: 1 minute | Serves 2 to 4

2 cups quinoa
3 cups water or vegetable broth
Juice of 1 lemon

½ teaspoon salt
Handful your choice of fresh herbs, minced

1. Rinse the quinoa well. 2. Add the quinoa, broth, lemon juice, salt, and, if using, herbs into the pressure cooker. 3. Close and lock the pressure cooker lid. Select Pressure Cook and set time to 1 minute at High pressure. Press Start. 4. When pressure cooking is complete, use a natural release for 10 minutes, then release any remaining pressure manually. 5. Carefully unlock the lid and fluff the cooked quinoa with a fork. 6. Serve.

Seafood Soup Stock

Prep time: 10 minutes | Cook time: 30 minutes | Serves 8

Shells and heads from ½ pound (227 g) prawns
8 cups water
4 onions, quartered
4 carrots, cut into chunks

3 cloves garlic, sliced
2 bay leaves
1 teaspoon whole black peppercorns

1. Put all of the ingredients into the pressure cooker. 2. Close and lock the pressure cooker lid. Select Pressure Cook and set time to 30 minutes at High pressure. Press Start. 3. When pressure cooking is complete, let the pressure release naturally for 15 minutes, and then release any remaining steam manually. Open the lid. 4. Strain the stock and pour into jars. Store in the refrigerator or freeze.

Chapter 3: Breakfasts

Maple-Pecan Steel-Cut Oats

Prep time: 5 minutes | Cook time: 4 minutes | Serves 4

2 cups steel-cut oats
3 cups water
1 (13½-ounce / 383-g) can full-fat coconut milk, divided
⅓ cup pure maple syrup, plus more to taste

½ teaspoon sea salt
½ cup toasted pecan pieces
2 teaspoons ground cinnamon (optional)

1. In the pressure cooker, combine the oats, water, 1 cup of the coconut milk, and the maple syrup and salt. Give the mixture a quick stir. Close and lock the pressure cooker lid. 2. Select Pressure Cook and set time to 4 minutes at High pressure. Press Start. 3. Use a natural release for 15 minutes, then release any remaining steam before removing the lid. 4. After removing the lid, stir in the remaining coconut milk and additional maple syrup to taste. 5. Serve with the toasted pecans and sprinkle with the cinnamon (if using).

Tomato and Spinach Breakfast

Prep time: 10 minutes | Cook time: 20 minutes | Serves 4 to 6

1½ cups water
12 beaten eggs
Salt and ground black pepper, to taste
½ cup milk
1 cup tomato, diced

3 cups baby spinach, chopped
3 green onions, sliced
4 tomato, sliced
¼ cup Parmesan, grated

1. Prepare the pressure cooker by adding the water to the pot and placing the steam rack in it. 2. In a bowl, mix the eggs with salt, pepper and milk. Stir to combine. 3. In a baking dish, mix diced tomato, spinach, and green onions. 4. Pour the eggs mix over veggies, spread tomato slices on top. Sprinkle with Parmesan. 5. Place the dish on the rack. 6. Close and lock the pressure cooker lid. Select Pressure Cook and set time to 20 minutes at High pressure. Press Start. 7. When pressure cooking is complete, use a quick release. Carefully uncover the pot. 8. If you want a crisp top, slide under the broiler for a few minutes at the end.

Cauliflower Avocado Toast

Prep time: 15 minutes | Cook time: 8 minutes | Serves 2

1 (12-ounce / 340-g) steamer bag cauliflower
1 large egg
½ cup shredded mozzarella cheese

1 ripe medium avocado
½ teaspoon garlic powder
¼ teaspoon ground black pepper

1. Cook cauliflower according to package instructions. Remove from bag and place into cheesecloth or clean towel to remove excess moisture. 2. Place cauliflower into a large bowl and mix in egg and mozzarella. Cut a piece of parchment to fit your air fryer basket. Separate the cauliflower mixture into two, and place it on the parchment in two mounds. Press out the cauliflower mounds into a ¼-inch-thick rectangle. Place the parchment into the air fryer basket. 3. Close and lock the air fryer lid. Select Air Fry, set temperature to 400°F (204°C), and set time to 8 minutes. Press Start. 4. Flip the cauliflower halfway through the cooking time. 5. When cooking is complete, remove the parchment and allow the cauliflower to cool 5 minutes. 6. Cut open the avocado and remove the pit. Scoop out the inside, place it in a medium bowl, and mash it with garlic powder and pepper. Spread onto the cauliflower. Serve immediately.

Peanut Butter and Chocolate Steel Cut Oats

Prep time: 2 minutes | Cook time: 12 minutes | Serves 4 to 6

2 cups steel cut oats
2½ cups water
2½ cups nondairy milk, divided, plus more as needed
¼ teaspoon salt

¼ cup vegan chocolate chips
¼ cup peanut butter
2 tablespoons agave, or maple syrup

1. In the pressure cooker, combine the oats, water, 2 cups of milk, the salt, and chocolate chips. Stir to mix. Close and lock the pressure cooker lid and turn the steam release handle to Sealing. Select Pressure Cook and set time to 12 minutes at High pressure. Press Start. 2. When pressure cooking is complete, turn off the pressure cooker. Let the pressure release naturally for 10 minutes; then release any remaining pressure manually. 3. Add the remaining ½ cup of milk (more if you want the oats thinner). Stir in the peanut butter and agave (I like my peanut butter in thick swirls!) and enjoy.

Breakfast Tacos with Pinto Beans and Tofu

Prep time: 20 minutes | Cook time: 30 minutes | Serves 4 to 6

2 tablespoons extra-virgin olive oil
3 cloves garlic, minced
1 yellow onion, diced
1 red, orange, or yellow bell pepper, seeded and diced
2 jalapeño chiles, seeded and diced
½ teaspoon fine sea salt
1 tablespoon chili powder
1 teaspoon ground cumin
½ teaspoon freshly ground black pepper
½ teaspoon ground turmeric
For Serving:
Sliced avocado
Chopped fresh cilantro

½ teaspoon dried oregano
1 cup low-sodium vegetable broth
1 (14-ounce / 397-g) block firm tofu, drained and crumbled
1½ cups cooked pinto beans, or 1 (15-ounce / 425-g) can beans, rinsed and drained
1 (14½-ounce / 411-g) can fire-roasted diced tomatoes
¼ cup nutritional yeast
12 warmed corn tortillas

Hot sauce

1. Select Sauté on the pressure cooker, add the oil and garlic, and heat for about 2 minutes, until the garlic is bubbling. Add the onion, bell pepper, jalapeños, and salt. Sauté for about 4 minutes, until the onion softens. 2. Add the chili powder, cumin, pepper, turmeric, and oregano and sauté for 1 minute more. Stir in the broth, using a wooden spoon to nudge loose any browned bits from the bottom of the pot. Stir in the tofu and beans, then pour the tomatoes and their liquid on top. Do not stir. 3. Close and lock the pressure cooker lid and set the pressure release to Sealing. Press the Cancel button to reset the cooking program. Then select Pressure Cook and set time to 10 minutes at High pressure. Press Start. (The pot will take about 15 minutes to come up to pressure before the cooking program begins.) 4. When the cooking program ends, perform a quick pressure release by moving the pressure release to Venting. Open the pot, add the nutritional yeast, and stir to combine. At this point, you can serve right away, or you can thicken the tofu mixture. 5. To thicken, press the Cancel button to reset the cooking program. Then select Sauté. Bring the tofu mixture to a simmer and cook, stirring occasionally, for 8 to 10 minutes, until thickened. Press the Cancel button to turn off the pot. 6. To serve, spoon the mixture onto the warmed tortillas. Top with avocado and cilantro and serve right away with hot sauce.

Blueberry Oatmeal

Prep time: 3 minutes | Cook time: 5 minutes | Serves 4

3 cups water
1½ cups frozen blueberries, divided
1 cup steel cut oats

1 tablespoon light brown sugar
⅛ teaspoon salt
½ teaspoon ground cinnamon

1. Combine water, 1 cup blueberries, oats, brown sugar, and salt in pressure cooker. Close and lock the pressure cooker lid and set pressure release to Sealing. 2. Press Pressure Cook button and set time to 5 minutes at High pressure. Press Start. 3. When pressure cooking is complete, allow pressure to release naturally for 10 minutes and then release remaining pressure manually. Unlock lid and remove it. 4. Top with cinnamon and remaining ½ cup blueberries and serve.

Pumpkin Donut Holes

Prep time: 15 minutes | Cook time: 14 minutes | Makes 12 donut holes

1 cup whole-wheat pastry flour, plus more as needed
3 tablespoons packed brown sugar
½ teaspoon ground cinnamon
1 teaspoon low-sodium baking powder
⅓ cup canned no-salt-added pumpkin purée (not

pumpkin pie filling)
3 tablespoons 2% milk, plus more as needed
2 tablespoons unsalted butter, melted
1 egg white
Powdered sugar (optional)

1. In a medium bowl, mix the pastry flour, brown sugar, cinnamon, and baking powder. 2. In a small bowl, beat the pumpkin, milk, butter, and egg white until combined. Add the pumpkin mixture to the dry ingredients and mix until combined. You may need to add more flour or milk to form a soft dough. 3. Divide the dough into 12 pieces. With floured hands, form each piece into a ball. 4. Cut a piece of parchment paper or aluminum foil to fit inside the air fryer basket but about 1 inch smaller in diameter. Poke holes in the paper or foil and place it in the basket. 5. Put 6 donut holes into the basket, leaving some space around each. Close and lock the air fryer lid. Select Air Fry, set temperature to 360°F (182°C), and set time to 7 minutes. Press Start. 6. Cook until the donut holes reach an internal temperature of 200°F (93°C) and are firm and light golden brown. Let cool for 5 minutes. Remove from the basket and roll in powdered sugar, if desired. Repeat with the remaining donut holes and serve.

Quick and Easy Blueberry Muffins

Prep time: 10 minutes | Cook time: 12 minutes | Makes 8 muffins

1⅓ cups flour
½ cup sugar
2 teaspoons baking powder
¼ teaspoon salt

⅓ cup canola oil
1 egg
½ cup milk
⅔ cup blueberries, fresh or frozen and thawed

1. In a medium bowl, stir together flour, sugar, baking powder, and salt. 2. In a separate bowl, combine oil, egg, and milk and mix well. 3. Add egg mixture to dry ingredients and stir just until moistened. 4. Gently stir in the blueberries. 5. Spoon batter evenly into parchment paper-lined muffin cups. 6. Put 4 muffin cups in air fryer basket. Close and lock the air fryer lid. Select Bake, set temperature to 330°F (166°C), and set time to 12 minutes. Press Start. 7. Cook until tops spring back when touched lightly. Repeat previous step to bake remaining muffins. 8. Serve immediately.

Cheddar Soufflés

Prep time: 15 minutes | Cook time: 12 minutes | Serves 4

3 large eggs, whites and yolks separated
¼ teaspoon cream of tartar

½ cup shredded sharp cheddar cheese
3 ounces (85 g) cream cheese, softened

1. In a large bowl, beat egg whites together with cream of tartar until soft peaks form, about 2 minutes. 2. In a separate medium bowl, beat egg yolks, cheddar, and cream cheese together until frothy, about 1 minute. Add egg yolk mixture to whites, gently folding until combined. 3. Pour mixture evenly into four ramekins greased with cooking spray. Place ramekins into air fryer basket. 4. Close and lock the air fryer lid. Select Bake, set temperature to 350ºF (177ºC), and set time to 12 minutes. Press Start. 5. Eggs will be browned on the top and firm in the center when done. Serve warm.

Mini Shrimp Frittata

Prep time: 15 minutes | Cook time: 20 minutes | Serves 4

1 teaspoon olive oil, plus more for spraying
½ small red bell pepper, finely diced
1 teaspoon minced garlic
1 (4-ounce / 113-g) can of tiny shrimp, drained

Salt and freshly ground black pepper, to taste
4 eggs, beaten
4 teaspoons ricotta cheese

1. Spray four ramekins with olive oil. 2. In a medium skillet over medium-low heat, heat 1 teaspoon of olive oil. Add the bell pepper and garlic and sauté until the pepper is soft, about 5 minutes 3. Add the shrimp, season with salt and pepper, and cook until warm, 1 to 2 minutes. Remove from the heat. 4. Add the eggs and stir to combine. 5. Pour one quarter of the mixture into each ramekin. 6. Place 2 ramekins in the air fryer basket. Close and lock the air fryer lid. Select Bake, set temperature to 350ºF (177ºC), and set time to 6 minutes. Press Start. 7. Remove the air fryer basket and stir the mixture in each ramekin. Top each fritatta with 1 teaspoon of ricotta cheese. Return the air fryer basket to the pressure cooker and cook until eggs are set and the top is lightly browned, 4 to 5 minutes. 8. Repeat with the remaining two ramekins.

Sunday Brunch Broccoli Egg Cups

Prep time: 10 minutes | Cook time: 6 minutes | Serves 4

7 large eggs
1½ cups half-and-half cream
3 tablespoons shredded Swiss cheese
2 teaspoons minced fresh parsley
1 teaspoon minced fresh basil

¼ teaspoon salt
⅛ teaspoon cayenne pepper
1 to 1½ cups frozen broccoli florets, thawed
1 cup water

1. Whisk three eggs with next six ingredients; pour into four greased 8-ounce (227-g) ramekins. Divide broccoli among ramekins; top each with one remaining egg. 2. Add 1 cup water and steam rack to pressure cooker. Place ramekins on rack, offset-stacking as needed, and covering loosely with foil. 3. Close and lock the pressure cooker lid; make sure vent is closed. Select Steam and set time to 6 minutes at High pressure. Press Start. When pressure cooking is complete, use a quick release. Remove lid; using tongs, carefully remove the ramekins. Let stand for 3 minutes before serving.

Cornmeal Mush

Prep time: 5 minutes | Cook time: 15 minutes | Serves 6

1 cup yellow cornmeal
4 cups water, divided

½ teaspoon salt
1 tablespoon vegan margarine

1. In a medium bowl, whisk together the cornmeal, 1 cup water, and salt. Set aside. 2. Add the remaining water to the pressure cooker and press the Sauté button. Bring to a boil. Stir the cornmeal and water mixture into the boiling water. Add the margarine and stir continuously until the mixture returns to a boil. 3. Close and lock the pressure cooker lid. Press the Pressure Cook button and set time to 10 minutes at High pressure. Press Start. When pressure cooking is complete, use a quick release and then unlock the lid. 4. Spoon into serving bowls and serve warm.

Homemade Granola

Prep time: 10 minutes | Cook time: 2 hours 30 minutes | Serves 6

4 cups old-fashioned rolled oats
1 cup roasted almonds, roughly chopped
¼ cup packed light brown sugar
½ teaspoon ground cinnamon
½ teaspoon salt

½ cup olive oil
½ cup honey
1 teaspoon vanilla extract
½ cup dried cranberries

1. Spray inside of pressure cooker with cooking spray. 2. Pour in rolled oats, almonds, brown sugar, cinnamon, and salt. Mix together. 3. In a small bowl, whisk together oil, honey, and vanilla. 4. Pour wet ingredients over dry ingredients in the pot and mix until fully combined. 5. Cover partially with the pressure cooker lid, leaving 3 inches of open air. 6. Press Slow Cook button and set time to 2½ hours at Low pressure. Press Start. Let cook, stirring every 30 minutes. 7. When pressure cooking is complete, remove lid and mix in cranberries. Remove granola from pressure cooker and spread onto a large baking pan. Let cool. 8. Pour cooled granola into an airtight container. Store at room temperature five to seven days.

Chapter 4: Snacks and Appetizers

Classic Baba Ghanoush

Prep time: 10 minutes | Cook time: 10 minutes | Makes 1½ cups

1 tablespoon sesame oil

1 large eggplant, peeled and diced

4 cloves garlic, peeled and minced

½ cup water

¼ cup chopped fresh parsley, divided

¼ teaspoon ground cumin

½ teaspoon salt

2 tablespoons fresh lemon juice

2 tablespoons tahini

1 tablespoon olive oil

¼ teaspoon paprika

1. Press the Sauté button on pressure cooker. Heat sesame oil. Add eggplant and stir-fry for 4 to 5 minutes until it softens. Add garlic and cook for an additional minute. Add water. Close and lock the pressure cooker lid. 2. Press the Pressure Cook button and set time to 4 minutes at High pressure. Press Start. When pressure cooking is complete, let pressure release naturally until float valve drops and then unlock lid. 3. Strain the cooked eggplant and garlic. Add to a food processor or blender along with ⅛ cup parsley, cumin, salt, lemon juice, and tahini. Pulse to process. Add the olive oil and process until smooth. Transfer to a serving dish and garnish with remaining ⅛ cup chopped parsley and sprinkle with paprika.

Veggie Sushi

Prep time: 20 minutes | Cook time: 3 minutes | Makes 4 rolls

2 cups dried sushi rice (such as Lundberg Family Farms Organic California Sushi Rice)

2 cups water

4 sheets sushi nori

1 large avocado, sliced

For Serving:

Soy sauce (or coconut aminos for gluten-free and soy-free)

1 red bell pepper, deseeded and cut into thin strips

2 Persian cucumbers, thinly sliced lengthwise

1 cup shredded carrot

Sea salt (optional), to taste

2 tablespoons toasted sesame seeds

Prepared wasabi (optional)

Pickled ginger (optional)

1. Rinse the rice in several changes of water until the water is clear. Drain and add the rice to the pressure cooker along with 2 cups water. 2. Close and lock the pressure cooker lid and ensure the steam release valve is set to the Sealing position. Select Pressure Cook and set time to 3 minutes at High pressure. Press Start. 3. When pressure cooking is complete, allow the pressure to release naturally. Carefully remove the lid and stir the rice. Transfer to a bowl to cool. 4. To make each sushi roll, lay one piece of nori on a bamboo sushi mat or on a piece of parchment paper slightly larger than the nori sheet. Cover the nori with a thin layer of rice (about 1 cup), leaving 1 inch bare at the top and bottom. Place a line of veggies along the edge closest to you. Sprinkle with a pinch of salt, if desired. Wrap that edge of nori over the veggies and continue to roll as tightly as possible until you form a log—use the bamboo mat or parchment to help to roll the sushi tightly. Seal the roll by brushing a little water where the edge meets the other side of the roll. 5. Use a very sharp chef's knife to cut the roll crosswise into 8 (1-inch) pieces. Sprinkle with sesame seeds. 6. Serve the sushi rolls immediately, or refrigerate until ready to eat. Serve with soy sauce or coconut aminos for dipping. Wasabi and pickled ginger add even more flavor for serving, but are optional.

Fried Peaches

Prep time: 15 minutes | Cook time: 6 to 8 minutes | Serves 4

2 egg whites

1 tablespoon water

¼ cup sliced almonds

2 tablespoons brown sugar

½ teaspoon almond extract

1 cup crisp rice cereal

2 medium, very firm peaches, peeled and pitted

¼ cup cornstarch

Oil for misting or cooking spray

1. Beat together egg whites and water in a shallow dish. 2. In a food processor, combine the almonds, brown sugar, and almond extract. Process until ingredients combine well and the nuts are finely chopped. 3. Add cereal and pulse just until cereal crushes. Pour crumb mixture into a shallow dish or onto a plate. 4. Cut each peach into eighths and place in a plastic bag or container with lid. Add cornstarch, seal, and shake to coat. 5. Remove peach slices from bag or container, tapping them hard to shake off the excess cornstarch. Dip in egg wash and roll in crumbs. Spray with oil. 6. Place in air fryer basket. Close and lock the air fryer lid. Select Air Fry, set temperature to 390°F (199°C), and set time to 5 minutes. Press Start. 7. Shake basket, separate any that have stuck together, and spritz a little oil on any spots that aren't browning. 8. Cook for 1 to 3 minutes longer, until golden brown and crispy.

Savoy Cabbage Rolls

Prep time: 20 minutes | Cook time: 20 minutes | Makes 20 rolls

1 medium head savoy cabbage

3 cups water, divided

½ pound (227 g) ground beef

1 cup long-grain rice

1 small red bell pepper, seeded and minced

1 medium onion, peeled and diced

1 cup beef broth

1 tablespoon olive oil

2 tablespoons minced fresh mint

1 teaspoon dried tarragon

1 teaspoon salt

½ teaspoon ground black pepper

2 tablespoons lemon juice

1. Wash the cabbage. Remove the large outer leaves and set aside. Remove remaining cabbage leaves and place them in the pressure cooker. Pour in 1 cup water. Close and lock the pressure cooker lid. 2. Press the Steam button and set time to 1 minute at Low pressure. Press Start. When pressure cooking is complete, use a quick release and then unlock lid. Drain the cabbage leaves in a colander and then move them to a cotton towel. 3. In a medium mixing bowl, add the ground beef, rice, bell pepper, onion, broth, olive oil, mint, tarragon, salt, and pepper. Stir to combine. 4. Place the reserved (uncooked) cabbage leaves on the bottom of the pressure cooker. 5. Remove the stem running down the center of each steamed cabbage leaf and tear each leaf in half lengthwise. Place 1 tablespoon of the ground beef mixture in the center of each cabbage piece. Loosely fold the sides of the leaf over the filling and then fold the top and bottom of the leaf over the folded sides. As you complete them, place each stuffed cabbage leaf in the pressure cooker. 6. Pour 2 cups water and the lemon juice over the stuffed cabbage rolls. Close and lock the pressure cooker lid. 7. Press the Pressure Cook button and set time to 15 minutes at High pressure. Press Start. When pressure cooking is complete, let pressure release naturally for 10 minutes. Release any remaining pressure manually and then unlock lid. 8. Carefully move the stuffed cabbage rolls to a serving platter. Serve warm.

Tangy Fried Pickle Spears

Prep time: 5 minutes | Cook time: 15 minutes | Serves 6

2 jars sweet and sour pickle spears, patted dry
2 medium-sized eggs
⅓ cup milk
1 teaspoon garlic powder
1 teaspoon sea salt

½ teaspoon shallot powder
⅓ teaspoon chili powder
⅓ cup all-purpose flour
Cooking spray

1. Spritz the air fryer basket with cooking spray. 2. In a bowl, beat together the eggs with milk. In another bowl, combine garlic powder, sea salt, shallot powder, chili powder and all-purpose flour until well blended. 3. One by one, roll the pickle spears in the powder mixture, then dredge them in the egg mixture. Dip them in the powder mixture a second time for additional coating. 4. Arrange the coated pickles in the prepared basket. Close and lock the air fryer lid. Select Air Fry, set temperature to 385°F (196°C), and set time to 15 minutes. Press Start. Cook until golden and crispy, shaking the basket halfway through to ensure even cooking. 5. Transfer to a plate and let cool for 5 minutes before serving.

Crispy Cajun Dill Pickle Chips

Prep time: 5 minutes | Cook time: 10 minutes | Makes 16 slices

¼ cup all-purpose flour
½ cup panko bread crumbs
1 large egg, beaten

2 teaspoons Cajun seasoning
2 large dill pickles, sliced into 8 rounds each
Cooking spray

1. Place the all-purpose flour, panko bread crumbs, and egg into 3 separate shallow bowls, then stir the Cajun seasoning into the flour. 2. Dredge each pickle chip in the flour mixture, then the egg, and finally the bread crumbs. Shake off any excess, then place each coated pickle chip on a plate. 3. Spritz the air fryer basket with cooking spray, then place 8 pickle chips in the basket. Close and lock the air fryer lid. Select Air Fry, set temperature to 390°F (199°C), and set time to 5 minutes. Press Start. Cook until crispy and golden brown. Repeat this process with the remaining pickle chips. 4. Remove the chips and allow to slightly cool on a wire rack before serving.

Kale Chips with Tex-Mex Dip

Prep time: 10 minutes | Cook time: 5 to 6 minutes | Serves 8

1 cup Greek yogurt
1 tablespoon chili powder
⅓ cup low-sodium salsa, well drained

1 bunch curly kale
1 teaspoon olive oil
¼ teaspoon coarse sea salt

1. In a small bowl, combine the yogurt, chili powder, and drained salsa; refrigerate. 2. Rinse the kale thoroughly, and pat dry. Remove the stems and ribs from the kale, using a sharp knife. Cut or tear the leaves into 3-inch pieces. 3. Toss the kale with the olive oil in a large bowl. 4. Place in air fryer basket. Close and lock the air fryer lid. Select Air Fry, set temperature to 390°F (199°C), and set time to 6 minutes. Press Start. Cook the kale in small batches until the leaves are crisp. This should take 5 to 6 minutes. Shake the basket once during cooking time. 5. As you remove the kale chips, sprinkle them with a bit of the sea salt. 6. When all of the kale chips are done, serve with the dip.

Cheesy Hash Brown Bruschetta

Prep time: 5 minutes | Cook time: 8 minutes | Serves 4

4 frozen hash brown patties
1 tablespoon olive oil
⅓ cup chopped cherry tomatoes
3 tablespoons diced fresh mozzarella

2 tablespoons grated Parmesan cheese
1 tablespoon balsamic vinegar
1 tablespoon minced fresh basil

1. Place the hash brown patties in the air fryer basket in a single layer. 2. Close and lock the air fryer lid. Select Air Fry, set temperature to 400ºF (204ºC), and set time to 8 minutes. Press Start. Cook until the potatoes are crisp, hot, and golden brown. 3. Meanwhile, combine the olive oil, tomatoes, mozzarella, Parmesan, vinegar, and basil in a small bowl. 4. When the potatoes are done, carefully remove from the basket and arrange on a serving plate. Top with the tomato mixture and serve.

Feta and Quinoa Stuffed Mushrooms

Prep time: 5 minutes | Cook time: 8 minutes | Serves 6

2 tablespoons finely diced red bell pepper
1 garlic clove, minced
¼ cup cooked quinoa
⅛ teaspoon salt
¼ teaspoon dried oregano

24 button mushrooms, stemmed
2 ounces (57 g) crumbled feta
3 tablespoons whole wheat bread crumbs
Olive oil cooking spray

1. In a small bowl, combine the bell pepper, garlic, quinoa, salt, and oregano. 2. Spoon the quinoa stuffing into the mushroom caps until just filled. 3. Add a small piece of feta to the top of each mushroom. 4. Sprinkle a pinch bread crumbs over the feta on each mushroom. 5. Spray the air fryer basket with olive oil cooking spray, then gently place the mushrooms into the basket, making sure that they don't touch each other. (Depending on the size of the basket, you may have to cook them in two batches.) 6. Close and lock the air fryer lid. Select Bake, set temperature to 360ºF (182ºC), and set time to 8 minutes. Press Start. 7. Remove from the basket and serve.

Rumaki

Prep time: 30 minutes | Cook time: 10 to 12 minutes per batch | Makes about 24 rumaki

10 ounces (283 g) raw chicken livers
1 can sliced water chestnuts, drained

¼ cup low-sodium teriyaki sauce
12 slices turkey bacon

1. Cut livers into 1½-inch pieces, trimming out tough veins as you slice. 2. Place livers, water chestnuts, and teriyaki sauce in small container with lid. If needed, add another tablespoon of teriyaki sauce to make sure livers are covered. Refrigerate for 1 hour. 3. When ready to cook, cut bacon slices in half crosswise. 4. Wrap 1 piece of liver and 1 slice of water chestnut in each bacon strip. Secure with toothpick. 5. When you have wrapped half of the livers, place them in the air fryer basket in a single layer. 6. Close and lock the air fryer lid. Select Air Fry, set temperature to 390ºF (199ºC), and set time to 12 minutes. Press Start. Cook until liver is done and bacon is crispy. 7. While first batch cooks, wrap the remaining livers. Repeat step 6 to cook your second batch.

Chapter 5: Beans and Grains

Almond Garlic Green Beans

Prep time: 5 minutes | Cook time: 5 minutes | Serves 4

1 teaspoon sesame oil

4 or 5 cloves garlic, thinly sliced lengthwise

1 pound (454 g) green beans, cut into ½-inch pieces

¼ cup water

¼ teaspoon sea salt

¼ cup almond slivers

1. In an uncovered pressure cooker, heat the oil. Add the garlic and sauté until soft, about 2 minutes. Add the green beans and water. 2. Close and lock the pressure cooker lid. Select Pressure Cook and set time to 1 minute at High pressure. Press Start. When pressure cooking is complete, use a quick release. 3. Remove the lid stir in the salt. Add the almond slivers, toss, and serve.

Szechuan String Beans

Prep time: 5 minutes | Cook time: 3 minutes | Serves 4 to 6

1½ pounds (680 g) green beans, ends trimmed

¼ cup vegetable or garlic broth

¼ cup low-sodium soy sauce

2 tablespoons almonds, chopped (optional)

3 cloves garlic, minced or pressed

2 tablespoons sesame oil

2 tablespoons sriracha

1 tablespoon rice vinegar

1 tablespoon paprika

2 teaspoons garlic powder

1 teaspoon onion powder

¼ teaspoon cayenne pepper (optional)

¼ teaspoon crushed red pepper flakes (optional)

1. Put all the ingredients in the pressure cooker and stir well. 2. Close and lock the pressure cooker lid, move the valve to the Sealing position, and select Pressure Cook and set time to 3 minutes at High pressure. Press Start. When pressure cooking is complete, use a quick release.

Feijoada

Prep time: 10 minutes | Cook time: 35 minutes | Serves 6 to 8

1 large onion, diced

3 or 4 garlic cloves, minced

1 tablespoon olive oil

2 cups dried black beans

4 cups water and/or unsalted vegetable broth

1 tablespoon ground cumin

1 tablespoon smoked paprika

1 tablespoon dried oregano

Salt

¼ cup fresh cilantro, chopped

1. On your pressure cooker, select Sauté. Add the onion, garlic, and olive oil. Cook for about 5 minutes, stirring occasionally, until the onion is softened. Add the black beans, water, cumin, paprika, and oregano, stirring to combine. Cancel Sauté. 2. Close and lock the pressure cooker lid and ensure the pressure valve is sealed, then select Pressure Cook and set time to 30 minutes at High pressure. Press Start. 3. When pressure cooking is complete, let the pressure release naturally, about 30 minutes. 4. Once all the pressure has released, carefully unlock and remove the lid. Taste and season with ½ to 1 teaspoon of salt. If your beans are not quite soft enough, or if you have too much liquid, select Sauté and cook, uncovered, for 10 to 15 minutes more. Stir in the cilantro just before serving.

White Beans with Rosemary and Garlic

Prep time: 10 minutes | Cook time: 30 minutes | Serves 8

1 pound (454 g) dry navy beans
6 cups vegetable broth
6 springs fresh rosemary
1 tablespoon onion powder

2 teaspoons garlic powder
½ teaspoon salt
1 bay leaf

1. Combine all ingredients in the pressure cooker. Close and lock the pressure cooker lid and set pressure release to Sealing. 2. Press Pressure Cook button and set time to 30 minutes at High pressure. Press Start. 3. When pressure cooking is complete, allow pressure to release naturally and then unlock lid and remove it. 4. Serve.

Cold Quinoa Salad with Fruit and Pecans

Prep time: 10 minutes | Cook time: 8 minutes | Serves 4 to 6

1 cup quinoa, rinsed
1 cup water
¼ teaspoon salt, plus more as needed
2 apples, unpeeled, cut into large dice
2 tablespoons freshly squeezed lemon juice
1 tablespoon white rice vinegar
½ bunch scallions, green and light green parts, sliced
2 celery stalks, halved lengthwise and chopped

¾ to 1 cup dried cranberries, white raisins, and regular raisins (many stores carry a mix like this in their bulk section)
½ to 1 teaspoon chili powder, plus more as needed
2 tablespoons avocado oil, or walnut oil
Pinch freshly ground black pepper
½ cup fresh cilantro, chopped
½ to 1 cup pecans, chopped

1. In your pressure cooker, combine the quinoa, water, and salt, and stir. Close and lock the pressure cooker lid and turn the steam release handle to Sealing. Select Pressure Cook and set time to 8 minutes at High pressure. Press Start. 2. When pressure cooking is complete, let the pressure release naturally for 10 minutes; then release the remaining pressure manually. 3. Carefully remove the lid and transfer the quinoa to a large bowl. Refrigerate for 5 minutes to cool. 4. In a small resealable container, combine the apples, lemon juice, and vinegar. Cover and shake lightly to coat the apples, then refrigerate. 5. Remove the cooled quinoa from the refrigerator and stir in the scallions, celery, cranberry-raisin mix, chili powder, and oil. Taste and season with more salt and pepper, as needed. Stir the apples and whatever lemon-vinegar juice is in the container into the salad. 6. Add the cilantro and pecans immediately before serving.

Restaurant-Style Pinto Beans

Prep time: 10 minutes | Cook time: 51 minutes | Serves 8

2 tablespoons olive oil
1 medium yellow onion, peeled and diced
4 cloves garlic, minced
4 cups chicken broth
1 pound (454 g) dry pinto beans

2 tablespoons chili powder
1 teaspoon cumin
1 teaspoon dried oregano
½ teaspoon salt
¼ teaspoon black pepper

1. Press Sauté button and add oil. Add in onion and fry 5 minutes, stirring occasionally. 2. Add in garlic and cook an additional 30 seconds. 3. Pour broth into pressure cooker and deglaze bottom of pot. Turn pressure cooker off. 4. Mix in beans, chili powder, cumin, oregano, salt, and pepper. 5. Close and lock the pressure cooker lid and set pressure release to Sealing. 6. Press Pressure Cook button and set time to 45 minutes at High pressure. Press Start. 7. When pressure cooking is complete, allow pressure to release naturally and then unlock lid and remove it. Serve.

Parmesan Risotto

Prep time: 5 minutes | Cook time: 20 minutes | Serves 4

4 tablespoons butter
1 small onion, peeled and finely diced
2 cloves garlic, minced
1½ cups Arborio rice

4 cups chicken broth, divided
3 tablespoons grated Parmesan cheese
½ teaspoon salt
¼ teaspoon ground black pepper
½ cup chopped fresh parsley

1. Press the Sauté button on pressure cooker. Add and melt the butter. Add the onion and stir-fry for 3 to 5 minutes until onions are translucent. Add garlic and rice and cook for an additional minute. Add 1 cup broth and stir for 2 to 3 minutes until it is absorbed by the rice. 2. Add remaining 3 cups broth, Parmesan cheese, salt, and pepper. Close and lock the pressure cooker lid. 3. Press the Pressure Cook button and set time to 10 minutes at High pressure. Press Start. When pressure cooking is complete, let pressure release naturally for 10 minutes. Release any remaining pressure manually and then unlock lid. 4. Ladle into bowls and garnish each with ⅛ cup fresh parsley.

Polenta with Black Pepper

Prep time: 5 minutes | Cook time: 20 minutes | Serves 4

4 cups low-sodium vegetable broth
3 tablespoons extra-virgin olive oil, plus more for serving
1 cup coarse polenta (not an instant or quick-cooking

variety)
¾ teaspoon freshly ground black pepper, plus more for serving
¼ teaspoon fine sea salt, plus more as needed

1. Select Sauté on the pressure cooker. Add the broth and oil, then cover the pot with the glass lid and cook just until it begins to simmer, 8 to 10 minutes. Whisking constantly, pour the polenta into the broth in a thin stream. Press the Cancel button to reset the cooking program. 2. Close and lock the pressure cooker lid and set the pressure release to Sealing. Select Pressure Cook and set time to 10 minutes at High pressure. Press Start. (The pot will take about 5 minutes to come up to pressure before the cooking program begins.) 3. When the cooking program ends, let the pressure release naturally for 15 minutes, then move the pressure release to Venting to release any remaining steam. Open the pot and, wearing heat-resistant mitts, lift out the inner pot. 4. The polenta will have some liquid on the top; stir to incorporate the liquid, using a wooden spoon to scrape along the bottom of the pot to loosen any stuck polenta. If there are any lumps, break them up with a whisk. Stir in the pepper and salt. Taste for seasoning and add more salt, if needed. 5. Spoon the polenta into bowls, drizzle with oil, and top with a few grinds of pepper. Serve piping hot.

Chicken Herb Rice

Prep time: 10 minutes | Cook time: 9 minutes | Serves 6

2 tablespoons olive oil
1½ cups dry white rice
1 medium yellow onion, peeled and diced
1 tablespoon dried parsley

1 teaspoon granulated sugar
½ teaspoon celery seed
¼ teaspoon salt
2 cups chicken broth

1. Press Sauté button and add oil. Add in rice and onion and fry 5 minutes, stirring occasionally. 2. Season with parsley, sugar, celery seed, and salt. Stir to combine. 3. Pour broth into pressure cooker and deglaze bottom of pot. Turn pressure cooker off. 4. Close and lock the pressure cooker lid and set pressure release to Sealing. 5. Press Pressure Cook button and set time to 4 minutes at High pressure. Press Start. 6. When pressure cooking is complete, allow pressure to release naturally for 10 minutes and then release the remaining pressure manually. Unlock lid and remove it. 7. Fluff rice with a fork and serve.

Chapter 6: Soups and Stews

Beet Soup

Prep time: 10 minutes | Cook time: 35 minutes | Serves 4

¾ pound (340 g) beets, peeled and chopped
4 cups chicken broth
1 onion, chopped

Salt and ground black pepper, to taste
¼ cup fresh basil leaves, chopped

1. Combine all of the ingredients in the pressure cooker and stir to mix. 2. Close and lock the pressure cooker lid. Select Pressure Cook and set time to 35 minutes at High pressure. Press Start. 3. When pressure cooking is complete, let the pressure release naturally for 10 minutes, then release any remaining steam manually. Open the lid. 4. With an immersion blender, blend the soup until smooth. 5. Taste for seasoning and add more salt if needed.

Wild Rice Soup

Prep time: 15 minutes | Cook time: 48 minutes | Serves 8

2 tablespoons unsalted butter
4 medium carrots, peeled and chopped
4 stalks celery, chopped
1 medium onion, peeled and chopped
1 (8-ounce / 227-g) container sliced mushrooms
2 cloves garlic, peeled and minced
½ teaspoon dried thyme

1 teaspoon salt
½ teaspoon black pepper
1 cup uncooked wild rice
4 cups chicken broth
⅓ cup water
2 tablespoons cornstarch
½ cup heavy cream

1. Press the Sauté button on the pressure cooker and melt butter. Add carrots, celery, and onion. Cook until vegetables are just tender, about 4 to 5 minutes, then add mushrooms and cook until they start to release liquid, about 3 minutes. 2. Add garlic, thyme, salt, pepper, and rice and cook until garlic is fragrant, about 1 minute. Press the Cancel button, add broth, and close lid. Set steam release to Sealing, select Pressure Cook and set time to 45 minutes at High pressure. Press Start. 3. When pressure cooking is complete, use a quick release, open lid, and stir well. Press the Cancel button, then press the Sauté button. Whisk together water and cornstarch and stir into pot. Bring to a boil, stirring constantly, until thickened, about 3 to 4 minutes. Press the Cancel button and stir in cream. Serve hot.

Creamy Celery Soup

Prep time: 20 minutes | Cook time: 1 minute | Serves 8

4 tablespoons unsalted butter
6 stalks celery, diced
1 medium onion, peeled and diced
1 clove garlic, peeled and minced
¼ teaspoon dried dill

½ teaspoon salt
¼ teaspoon ground black pepper
¼ cup all-purpose flour
4 cups chicken broth
½ cup heavy whipping cream

1. Press the Sauté button and melt butter. Add celery and onion. Cook until tender, about 8 minutes, then add garlic, dill, salt, and pepper. Cook until fragrant, about 1 minute. 2. Add flour and cook for 1 minute, making sure all flour is moistened. Press the Cancel button, then slowly add broth and mix well, scraping the bottom of pot well. Close and lock the pressure cooker lid, set steam release to Sealing, select Pressure Cook and set time to 1 minute at High pressure. Press Start. 3. When pressure cooking is complete, let pressure release naturally for 10 minutes, then use a quick release. Press the Cancel button and open lid. Purée soup with an immersion blender or blend soup in batches in a blender. Stir in cream. Serve hot.

Beef Noodle Soup

Prep time: 30 minutes | Cook time: 24 minutes | Serves 8

2 pounds (907 g) boneless chuck roast, cut into 1-inch pieces
¼ cup all-purpose flour
1 teaspoon salt, divided
1 teaspoon ground black pepper, divided
2 tablespoons vegetable oil, divided
2 medium yellow onions, peeled and chopped
2 medium carrots, peeled and chopped

2 stalks celery, chopped
2 cloves garlic, peeled and minced
1 tablespoon tomato paste
¼ teaspoon dried thyme
1 (14-ounce / 397-g) can diced tomatoes, undrained
4 cups beef broth
2 cups water
4 ounces (113 g) elbow macaroni

1. Place beef, flour, and ½ teaspoon each salt and pepper in a large zip-top plastic bag. Shake well, making sure beef is evenly coated. 2. Press the Sauté button on the pressure cooker and heat 1 tablespoon oil. Add half of the beef to pot, making sure there is a little space between each piece. Brown for 2 to 3 minutes per side. Transfer beef to a plate and repeat with remaining oil and beef. 3. Add onions, carrots, and celery to pot. Cook until just tender, about 5 minutes. Add garlic, tomato paste, and thyme and cook until fragrant, about 1 minute. Press the Cancel button. 4. Return beef to pot. Add tomatoes, broth, and water. Stir well, making sure to scrape up any bits on the bottom of pot. Close and lock the pressure cooker lid, set steam release to Sealing, select Pressure Cook and set time to 20 minutes at High pressure. Press Start. 5. When pressure cooking is complete, let pressure release naturally, about 15 minutes. Open lid and stir in remaining ½ teaspoon each salt and pepper. Press the Cancel button. 6. Add macaroni to pot and stir well. Close and lock the pressure cooker lid, set steam release to Sealing, select Pressure Cook and set time to 4 minutes at High pressure. Press Start. When pressure cooking is complete, use a quick release. Open lid and stir well. Serve hot.

Crawfish Gumbo

Prep time: 30 minutes | Cook time: 18 minutes | Serves 8

¼ cup vegetable oil
¼ cup all-purpose flour
4 stalks celery, chopped
1 large yellow onion, peeled and diced
1 green bell pepper, seeded and diced
3 cloves garlic, minced
1 (15-ounce / 425-g) can diced tomatoes
½ teaspoon thyme
½ teaspoon Creole seasoning
3 bay leaves

2 tablespoons fileé powder
2 tablespoons Worcestershire sauce
1 teaspoon hot sauce
4 cups chicken broth
1 pound (454 g) smoked sausage, sliced
2 cups parboiled crawfish tails
¼ teaspoon salt
¼ teaspoon ground black pepper
2 cups cooked long-grain rice

1. Press the Sauté button on the pressure cooker and heat oil. Add flour and cook, stirring constantly, until flour is medium brown in color, about 15 minutes. 2. Add celery, onion, green pepper, garlic, and tomatoes and cook, stirring constantly, until the vegetables are tender, about 8 minutes. Add thyme, Creole seasoning, bay leaves, fileé, Worcestershire sauce, hot sauce, and broth and stir well, making sure nothing is stuck to the bottom of the pot, then add sausage. Press the Cancel button. 3. Close and lock the pressure cooker lid and set steam release to Sealing, then press the Pressure Cook button and set time to to 8 minutes at High pressure. Press Start. When pressure cooking is complete, use a quick release. Open lid and stir in crawfish, salt, and black pepper, then let stand on the Keep Warm setting for 10 minutes. Discard bay leaves. Serve hot over rice.

Creamed Potato Leek Soup

Prep time: 20 minutes | Cook time: 20 minutes | Serves 8

4 tablespoons unsalted butter
2 medium leeks, thinly sliced
4 large russet potatoes, peeled and diced
1 clove garlic, minced
½ teaspoon dried thyme
½ teaspoon salt

1 bay leaf
¼ teaspoon ground black pepper
4 cups chicken broth
1 cup heavy whipping cream
¼ cup sliced scallions

1. Press the Sauté button on the pressure cooker and melt butter. Add leeks and cook until tender, about 8 minutes, then add potatoes, garlic, thyme, salt, bay leaf, and pepper. Cook until fragrant, about 1 minute. 2. Press the Cancel button, then slowly add broth and mix well. Close and lock the pressure cooker lid, set steam release to Sealing, select Pressure Cook and set time to 20 minutes at High pressure. Press Start. 3. When pressure cooking is complete, let pressure release naturally for 10 minutes, then use a quick release. Press the Cancel button, open lid, remove bay leaf, and purée soup with an immersion blender or blend soup in batches in a blender. Once smooth stir in cream. Serve hot with scallions for garnish.

Vietnamese Chicken Phở

Prep time: 20 minutes | Cook time: 6 minutes | Serves 6

1 tablespoon vegetable oil
1 medium onion, peeled and cut in half
1 (1-inch) piece ginger, peeled
6 cloves garlic, crushed
¼ cup chopped cilantro
1 medium Fuji apple, peeled, cored, and diced
2 star anise
3 cardamom pods, crushed
1 cinnamon stick
1 teaspoon coriander seeds
2 whole cloves
1 teaspoon salt
1 teaspoon whole black peppercorns

4 cups chicken stock
1 pound (454 g) bone-in, skin-on chicken thighs
2 tablespoons fish sauce
2 tablespoons soy sauce
1 tablespoon sugar
12 ounces (340 g) rice noodles, soaked in warm water for 30 minutes and drained
½ pound (227 g) cooked flank steak, thinly sliced
1 cup fresh mint leaves
1 cup fresh basil leaves
1 cup fresh bean sprouts
2 small jalapeño peppers, seeded and sliced
4 scallions, cut into 1-inch pieces

1. Press the Sauté button on the pressure cooker and heat oil. Add onion and ginger, cut sides down, to pot. Cook until onion and ginger start to brown, about 5 minutes, then remove from pot. Add garlic, cilantro, apple, star anise, cardamom, cinnamon, coriander, cloves, salt, and peppercorns to pot and toast until fragrant, about 2 minutes. Return onion and ginger to pot, add stock and stir well. Add chicken thighs to pot. Press the Cancel button. 2. Close and lock the pressure cooker lid, set steam release to Sealing, select Pressure Cook and set time to 6 minutes at High pressure. Press Start. When pressure cooking is complete, let pressure release naturally, about 20 minutes. Open lid and stir in fish sauce, soy sauce, and sugar. Transfer chicken thighs to cutting board. Remove skin from chicken and cut meat from bones. Set aside. Strain broth through a colander lined with cheesecloth, then return broth to pot and select Keep Warm. 3. To serve, ladle noodles into serving bowls. Top noodles with chicken, hot broth, and sliced steak. Serve with mint, basil, bean sprouts, jalapeños, and scallions on the side so you and your guests can add them as desired to the soup.

Thai Coconut-Chickpea Stew

Prep time: 10 minutes | Cook time: 3 minutes | Serves 4 to 5

8 ounces (227 g) mushrooms, sliced (about 3 cups)

3 cups cooked chickpeas (from 1 cup dried)

1 red bell pepper, seeded and chopped

1 (13½-ounce / 383-g) can coconut milk

2 tablespoons tamari or soy sauce

1 teaspoon Thai chili paste

1 teaspoon ground ginger

Salt, to taste

1. In your pressure cooker, combine the mushrooms, chickpeas, red bell pepper, coconut milk, tamari, chili paste, and ginger. Close and lock the pressure cooker lid and ensure the pressure valve is sealed, then select Select Pressure Cook and set time to 3 minutes at High pressure. Press Start. 2. When pressure cooking is complete, let the pressure release naturally, about 20 minutes, or quick release it, being careful not to get your fingers or face near the steam release. 3. Once all the pressure has released, carefully unlock and remove the lid. Taste and season with salt.

Chapter 7: Vegetables and Sides

Garlic Roasted Potatoes

Prep time: 2 minutes | Cook time: 17 minutes | Serves 4 to 6

5 tablespoons vegetable oil
5 cloves garlic
2 pounds (907 g) baby potatoes

1 rosemary spring
½ cup stock
Salt and ground black pepper, to taste

1. Select Sauté on the pressure cooker and heat the oil. 2. Add the garlic, potatoes and rosemary. 3. Cook, stirring occasionally, for 10 minutes or until the potatoes start to brown. 4. Using a fork, pierce the middle of each potato. 5. Pour in the stock. Season with salt and pepper. Stir well. 6. Press the Cancel button to stop the Sauté function. 7. Close and lock the pressure cooker lid. Select Pressure Cook and set time to 7 minutes at High pressure. Press Start. 8. When pressure cooking is complete, use a quick release. Carefully unlock the lid. 9. Serve.

Crustless Veggie Potpie

Prep time: 10 minutes | Cook time: 12 minutes | Serves 4

1 large head cauliflower, cut into florets
3 cups vegetable or chicken stock
1 cup frozen peas
2 cups sliced carrot
2 medium Yukon gold potatoes, peeled and diced
3 celery ribs, diced

1 medium yellow onion, diced
3 cloves garlic, minced
2 bay leaves
1½ teaspoons sea salt, plus more to taste
½ teaspoon dried marjoram
2 tablespoons fresh thyme, for garnish (optional)

1. In the pressure cooker, combine the cauliflower florets and stock. 2. Close and lock the pressure cooker lid. Select Pressure Cook and set time to 5 minutes at High pressure. Press Start. 3. Use a quick release and remove the lid. Using an immersion blender or blender, purée the cauliflower mixture to form the base of your potpie. (Place the mixture back in the pot if it was removed to blend.) 4. Add the frozen peas, carrot, potatoes, celery, onion, garlic and bay leaves to the cauliflower mixture. Sprinkle with the salt and marjoram and give the mixture a stir. 5. Close and lock the pressure cooker lid. Select Pressure Cook and set time to 7 minutes at High pressure. Press Start. Use a quick release and remove the lid. 6. Serve hot and garnish with fresh thyme (if using), and additional salt to taste (if needed).

Sweet and Sour Beet Salad

Prep time: 15 minutes | Cook time: 20 minutes | Serves 8

6 medium fresh beets (about 2 pounds / 907 g)
1½ cups water
¼ cup extra-virgin olive oil
3 tablespoons lemon juice
2 tablespoons cider vinegar

2 tablespoons honey
¼ teaspoon salt
¼ teaspoon pepper
2 large ruby red grapefruit, peeled and sectioned
2 small red onions, halved and thinly sliced

1. Scrub beets, trimming tops to 1 inch. Place beets on the steam rack of pressure cooker. Add 1½ cups water. Close and lock the pressure cooker lid; make sure vent is closed. Select Pressure Cook and set time to 20 minutes at High pressure. Press Start. 2. When pressure cooking is complete, let pressure release naturally before opening; remove beets and cool completely before peeling, halving and thinly slicing them. Place in a serving bowl. Whisk together next six ingredients. Pour over beets; add grapefruit and onion. Toss gently to coat.

Citrus-Roasted Broccoli Florets

Prep time: 5 minutes | Cook time: 12 minutes | Serves 6

4 cups broccoli florets (approximately 1 large head)
2 tablespoons olive oil
½ teaspoon salt

½ cup orange juice
1 tablespoon raw honey
Orange wedges, for serving (optional)

1. In a large bowl, combine the broccoli, olive oil, salt, orange juice, and honey. Toss the broccoli in the liquid until well coated. 2. Pour the broccoli mixture into the air fryer basket. Close and lock the air fryer lid. Select Roast, set temperature to 360ºF (182ºC), and set time to 12 minutes. Press Start. Roast for 6 minutes. Stir and roast for 6 minutes more. 3. Serve alone or with orange wedges for additional citrus flavor, if desired.

Buttery Green Beans

Prep time: 5 minutes | Cook time: 8 to 10 minutes | Serves 6

1 pound (454 g) green beans, trimmed
1 tablespoon avocado oil
1 teaspoon garlic powder

Sea salt and freshly ground black pepper, to taste
¼ cup (4 tablespoons) unsalted butter, melted
¼ cup freshly grated Parmesan cheese

1. In a large bowl, toss together the green beans, avocado oil, and garlic powder and season with salt and pepper. 2. Arrange the green beans in a single layer in the air fryer basket. Close and lock the air fryer lid. Select Air Fry, set temperature to 400ºF (204ºC), and set time to 8 to 10 minutes. Press Start. Toss halfway through. 3. Transfer the beans to a large bowl and toss with the melted butter. Top with the Parmesan cheese and serve warm.

Creamy Bacon-Corn Casserole

Prep time: 10 minutes | Cook time: 17 minutes | Serves 4

6 slices bacon, quartered
1 small red bell pepper, seeded and diced
¼ cup whole milk
2 tablespoons gluten-free all-purpose flour
2 tablespoons melted unsalted butter
2 ounces (57 g) cream cheese

½ teaspoon salt
½ teaspoon ground black pepper
2 (15¼-ounce / 432-g) cans corn, drained
2 tablespoons Parmesan cheese
1 cup water

1. Press the Sauté button on the pressure cooker. Add bacon to pot and cook 5 minutes until crisp. Transfer bacon to a paper towel-lined plate. Crumble when cooled. 2. Add bell pepper to pot and cook 5 minutes in bacon drippings until tender. 3. In medium bowl, whisk together milk and flour. Add butter, cream cheese, salt, and pepper. Add crumbled bacon, bell pepper, and corn. 4. Transfer to a 7-cup glass dish. Sprinkle with Parmesan cheese. 5. Add water to the pressure cooker. Close and lock the pressure cooker lid. 6. Press the Pressure Cook button and set time to 7 minutes at High pressure. Press Start. When pressure cooking is complete, let pressure release naturally for 5 minutes. Release any remaining pressure manually and then unlock lid. 7. Remove dish from the pressure cooker and let cool for 10 minutes. Serve warm.

Dijon Roast Cabbage

Prep time: 10 minutes | Cook time: 10 minutes | Serves 4

1 small head cabbage, cored and sliced into 1-inch-thick slices
2 tablespoons olive oil, divided
½ teaspoon salt

1 tablespoon Dijon mustard
1 teaspoon apple cider vinegar
1 teaspoon granular erythritol

1. Drizzle each cabbage slice with 1 tablespoon olive oil, then sprinkle with salt. Place slices into ungreased air fryer basket, working in batches if needed. Close and lock the air fryer lid. Select Air Fry, set temperature to 350°F (177°C), and set time to 10 minutes. Press Start. Cabbage will be tender and edges will begin to brown when done.
2. In a small bowl, whisk remaining olive oil with mustard, vinegar, and erythritol. Drizzle over cabbage in a large serving dish. Serve warm.

Asian-Inspired Roasted Broccoli

Prep time: 10 minutes | Cook time: 15 minutes | Serves 4

Broccoli:
Oil, for spraying
1 pound (454 g) broccoli florets
2 teaspoons peanut oil
Sauce:
2 tablespoons soy sauce
2 teaspoons honey

1 tablespoon minced garlic
½ teaspoon salt

2 teaspoons Sriracha
1 teaspoon rice vinegar

Make the Broccoli: 1. Line the air fryer basket with parchment and spray lightly with oil. 2. In a large bowl, toss together the broccoli, peanut oil, garlic, and salt until evenly coated. 3. Spread out the broccoli in an even layer in the prepared basket. 4. Close and lock the air fryer lid. Select Air Fry, set temperature to 400°F (204°C), and set time to 15 minutes. Press Start. Stir halfway through. **Make the Sauce:** 5. Meanwhile, in a small microwave-safe bowl, combine the soy sauce, honey, Sriracha, and rice vinegar and microwave on high for about 15 seconds. Stir to combine. 6. Transfer the broccoli to a serving bowl and add the sauce. Gently toss until evenly coated and serve immediately.

Roasted Garlic

Prep time: 5 minutes | Cook time: 20 minutes | Makes 12 cloves

1 medium head garlic

2 teaspoons avocado oil

1. Remove any hanging excess peel from the garlic but leave the cloves covered. Cut off ¼ of the head of garlic, exposing the tips of the cloves. 2. Drizzle with avocado oil. Place the garlic head into a small sheet of aluminum foil, completely enclosing it. Place it into the air fryer basket. 3. Close and lock the air fryer lid. Select Air Fry, set temperature to 400°F (204°C), and set time to 20 minutes. Press Start. If your garlic head is a bit smaller, check it after 15 minutes. 4. When done, garlic should be golden brown and very soft. 5. To serve, cloves should pop out and easily be spread or sliced. Store in an airtight container in the refrigerator up to 5 days. You may also freeze individual cloves on a baking sheet, then store together in a freezer-safe storage bag once frozen.

Green Beans with Shallots

Prep time: 5 minutes | Cook time: 6 minutes | Serves 4

1 cup water

¾ teaspoon salt, divided

1 pound (454 g) green beans, trimmed

2 tablespoons olive oil

1 medium shallot, peeled and minced

½ teaspoon black pepper

1. Pour water and ½ teaspoon salt into pressure cooker and add steam rack. Place green beans on top of steam rack. 2. Close and lock the pressure cooker lid and set pressure release to Sealing. 3. Press Steam button and set time to 0 minutes at High pressure. Press Start. 4. When pressure cooking is complete, quick release pressure and then unlock lid and remove it. Remove green beans. Drain water. 5. Press Sauté button and add oil to the pot. 6. Add shallot and green beans. Let cook, stirring occasionally, 6 minutes. 7. Season with remaining ¼ teaspoon salt and pepper. Remove from heat and serve.

Buttered Egg Noodles

Prep time: 2 minutes | Cook time: 4 minutes | Serves 6

1 (12-ounce / 340-g) bag egg noodles

3 tablespoons butter

¼ cup grated Parmesan cheese

½ teaspoon sea salt

¼ teaspoon ground black pepper

¼ cup chopped fresh parsley

1. Place noodles in an even layer in pressure cooker. Pour enough water to come about ¼ inch over pasta. Close and lock the pressure cooker lid. 2. Press the Pressure Cook button and set time to 4 minutes at High pressure. Press Start. When pressure cooking is complete, unplug the pressure cooker and let pressure release naturally for 3 minutes. Release any remaining pressure manually and then unlock lid. 3. Drain any residual water. Toss pasta with butter, Parmesan cheese, salt, pepper, and parsley. Serve immediately.

Chipotle Baked Beans

Prep time: 10 minutes | Cook time: 40 minutes | Serves 6

2 cups water

1 medium onion, chopped

2 teaspoons garlic powder

1 cup barbecue sauce

¾ cup light brown sugar

2 to 4 chipotle peppers, minced

1 pound (454 g) dried great northern beans

1 ham bone

1. In a medium bowl, whisk together the water, onion, garlic powder, barbecue sauce, brown sugar and chipotle peppers. Pour into the pressure cooker, then stir in the beans. Nestle the ham bone into the bean mixture. 2. Select Pressure Cook and set time to 40 minutes at High pressure. Press Start. 3. When pressure cooking is complete, quick release the pressure and carefully remove the lid. Remove the ham bone and allow to cool slightly, then remove any meat from the bone and return it to the pot. Stir well and serve.

Not-Baked Sweet Potatoes

Prep time: 3 minutes | Cook time: 10 to 20 minutes | Serves 4

4 whole sweet potatoes, washed well

1. Place the steam rack in your pressure cooker and add 1½ cups water. Place the sweet potatoes on the rack. Close and lock the pressure cooker lid. Select Pressure Cook and set time to 10 to 20 minutes at High pressure. This depends on their size: if the sweet potatoes are fairly thin, start them at 10 minutes; if they are really large, begin at 20 minutes. Press Start. 2. When pressure cooking is complete, let the pressure release naturally.

Air Fried Potatoes with Olives

Prep time: 15 minutes | Cook time: 40 minutes | Serves 1

1 medium russet potatoes, scrubbed and peeled
1 teaspoon olive oil
¼ teaspoon onion powder
⅛ teaspoon salt

Dollop of butter
Dollop of cream cheese
1 tablespoon Kalamata olives
1 tablespoon chopped chives

1. In a bowl, coat the potatoes with the onion powder, salt, olive oil, and butter. 2. Transfer to the air fryer basket. Close and lock the air fryer lid. Select Air Fry, set temperature to 400°F (204°C), and set time to 40 minutes. Press Start. Turn the potatoes over at the halfway point. 3. Take care when removing the potatoes from the basket and serve with the cream cheese, Kalamata olives and chives on top.

Cheesy Bacon Spaghetti Squash

Prep time: 10 minutes | Cook time: 10 minutes | Serves 4

1 large spaghetti squash (3½ pounds / 1.6 kg)
1 cup water
4 bacon strips, chopped
3 tablespoons butter

1 tablespoon brown sugar
½ teaspoon salt
¼ teaspoon pepper
½ cup shredded Swiss cheese

1. Halve squash lengthwise; discard seeds. Place squash, cut side down, on the steam rack of pressure cooker. Add water to cooker; insert steam rack. Close and lock the pressure cooker lid; make sure vent is closed. Select Steam and set time to 7 minutes at High pressure. Press Start. When pressure cooking is complete, use a quick release. Set aside; remove squash, rack and water from cooker. 2. Select Sauté; add bacon, stirring occasionally, and cook until crisp. With a slotted spoon, remove bacon to paper towels; reserve drippings. Stir in butter, brown sugar, salt and pepper. Separate squash strands with a fork and add to cooker; toss and heat through. Remove from heat. Stir in cheese, and place in a serving bowl. Top with bacon.

Chapter 8: Beef, Pork, and Lamb

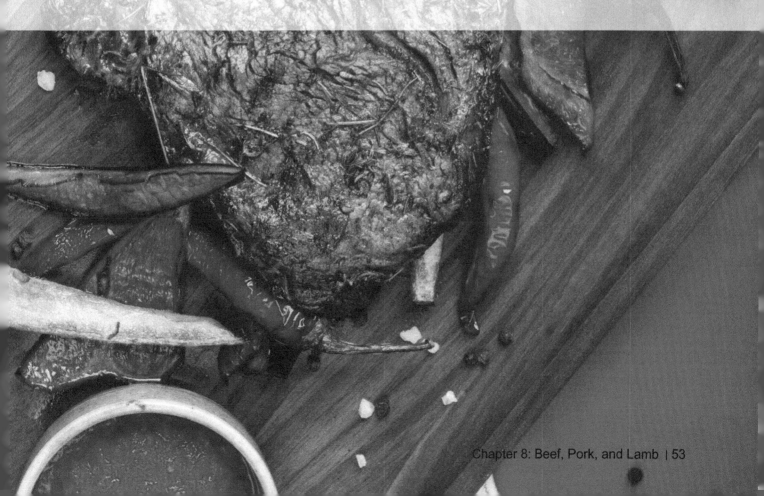

Meatballs with Asian Sauce

Prep time: 20 minutes | Cook time: 29 minutes | Serves 4

Sauce:

¼ cup tamari

¼ cup honey

⅛ cup rice vinegar

Meatballs:

½ pound (227 g) ground beef

½ pound (227 g) ground pork

1 large egg

1 medium shallot, peeled and finely diced

1 teaspoon sriracha

1-inch knob ginger, peeled and sliced

2 teaspoons sesame oil

1 tablespoon Chinese five-spice powder

3 tablespoons sesame oil, divided

2 cups water

1. In a small bowl, combine sauce ingredients. Set aside. 2. In a medium bowl, combine beef, pork, egg, shallot, and Chinese five-spice powder. Form mixture into twenty meatballs. Set aside. 3. Press the Sauté button on the pressure cooker and warm 2 tablespoons oil 30 seconds. Place ten meatballs around the edge of pot. Sear meatballs 4 minutes, making sure to get each side. Set aside. Add 1 tablespoon oil to pot and sear remaining meatballs 4 minutes. 4. Transfer seared meatballs to a 7-cup glass dish. Top with sauce. 5. Discard extra juice and oil from the pressure cooker. Add water to pot. Insert steam rack. Place the glass dish on top of the steam rack. Close and lock the pressure cooker lid. 6. Press the Pressure Cook button and set time to 20 minutes at High pressure. Press Start. When pressure cooking is complete, let pressure release naturally for 10 minutes. Release any remaining pressure manually and then unlock lid. 7. Transfer meatballs to a serving dish and serve warm.

Beef Pot Roast and Potatoes

Prep time: 20 minutes | Cook time: 1 hour | Serves 2

1 tablespoon oil

1½ pounds (680 g) lean beef shoulder roast, trimmed

Kosher salt

Freshly ground black pepper

1 medium onion, chopped

3 garlic cloves, crushed

2 large carrots, peeled and chopped

12 ounces (340 g) fingerling potatoes

2 cups beef stock

1 tablespoon Worcestershire sauce

1 tablespoon cornstarch

Fresh thyme, for garnish

1. Preheat the pressure cooker on Sauté mode. When the display reads hot, add the oil. Season the roast with salt and pepper and use tongs to lower it into the pot. Sear on all sides, 3 to 4 minutes each side. Press Cancel. 2. Arrange the onion, garlic, carrots, and potatoes around the roast. Pour in the stock and add the Worcestershire sauce. 3. Close and lock the pressure cooker lid. Select Pressure Cook and set time to 60 minutes at High pressure. Press Start. Allow the pressure to naturally release, about 10 minutes. Open the vent at the top and remove the lid. Press Cancel. 4. Transfer the roast and vegetables to a serving platter. Let rest while you make the gravy. Strain the beef stock into a bowl, discarding the fat solids. Return all but 2 tablespoons of the stock to the pot and select Sauté. Whisk the cornstarch into the reserved stock in the bowl, then stir the slurry into the pot and bring to a simmer, stirring often, for 5 minutes, or until thickened. Taste and season with more salt, pepper, or Worcestershire sauce if desired. Pour the gravy into a gravy boat. 5. Serve the pot roast and veggies with the gravy and garnish with fresh thyme.

Shredded Beef Lettuce Cups

Prep time: 20 minutes | Cook time: 45 minutes | Serves 8

3 medium carrots, chopped

2 medium sweet red peppers, chopped

1 medium onion, chopped

1 boneless beef chuck roast

1 (8-ounce / 227-g) can unsweetened crushed pineapple, undrained

½ cup reduced-sodium soy sauce

2 tablespoons brown sugar

2 tablespoons white vinegar

1 garlic clove, minced

½ teaspoon pepper

3 tablespoons cornstarch

3 tablespoons water

24 Bibb or Boston lettuce leaves

Sliced green onions (optional)

1. Combine carrots, red peppers and onion in pressure cooker. Top with roast. In a small bowl, combine pineapple, soy sauce, brown sugar, vinegar, garlic and pepper; pour over roast. 2. Close and lock the pressure cooker lid. Select Pressure Cook and set time to 40 minutes at High pressure. Press Start. Let pressure release naturally. Press Cancel. Remove roast from pressure cooker. Cool slightly; shred roast with 2 forks. 3. Skim fat from cooking juices; return juices and vegetables to pressure cooker. In a small bowl, mix cornstarch and water until smooth; stir into pressure cooker. Select Sauté. Simmer, stirring constantly, until thickened, 1 to 2 minutes. Return shredded meat to pressure cooker; heat through. 4. Serve in lettuce leaves. If desired, sprinkle with onions.

Beef Chuck Cheeseburgers

Prep time: 10 minutes | Cook time: 11 minutes | Serves 4

¾ pound (340 g) ground beef chuck

1 envelope onion soup mix

Kosher salt and freshly ground black pepper, to taste

1 teaspoon paprika

4 slices Monterey Jack cheese

4 ciabatta rolls

1. In a bowl, stir together the ground chuck, onion soup mix, salt, black pepper, and paprika to combine well. 2. Take four equal portions of the mixture and mold each one into a patty. 3. Transfer to the air fryer basket. Close and lock the air fryer lid. Select Air Fry, set temperature to 385ºF (196ºC), and set time to 10 minutes. Press Start. 4. Put the slices of cheese on the top of the burgers. 5. Air fry for another minute before serving on ciabatta rolls.

Spice-Rubbed Pork Loin

Prep time: 5 minutes | Cook time: 20 minutes | Serves 6

1 teaspoon paprika

½ teaspoon ground cumin

½ teaspoon chili powder

½ teaspoon garlic powder

2 tablespoons coconut oil

1 (1½-pound / 680-g) boneless pork loin

½ teaspoon salt

¼ teaspoon ground black pepper

1. In a small bowl, mix paprika, cumin, chili powder, and garlic powder. 2. Drizzle coconut oil over pork. Sprinkle pork loin with salt and pepper, then rub spice mixture evenly on all sides. Place pork loin into ungreased air fryer basket. 3. Close and lock the air fryer lid. Select Air Fry, set temperature to 400ºF (204ºC), and set time to 20 minutes. Press Start. Turn pork halfway through cooking. Pork loin will be browned and have an internal temperature of at least 145ºF (63ºC) when done. Serve warm.

Pork Chops with Mushroom Gravy

Prep time: 10 minutes | Cook time: 8 minutes | Serves 2

1 tablespoon oil

2 bone-in, medium-cut pork chops

Kosher salt

Freshly ground black pepper

½ small onion, sliced

4 ounces (113 g) cremini mushrooms, sliced

2 garlic cloves, minced

Splash of dry white wine

1 cup chicken stock

1 tablespoon cornstarch

¾ cup sour cream

1 tablespoon butter

1. Preheat the pressure cooker on Sauté mode. When the display reads hot, add the oil. Season the pork chops generously with salt and pepper, sear on both sides, and transfer to a plate. 2. Add the onion, mushrooms, and garlic and sauté until softened, 3 minutes. Pour in the white wine and deglaze the pot, scraping up any browned bits from the bottom with a wooden spoon and stirring them into the liquid. 3. Add the stock and stir. Set the seared pork chops in the pot. Close and lock the pressure cooker lid. Select Pressure Cook and set time to 8 minutes at High pressure. Press Start. Allow the pressure to naturally release, about 10 minutes. Open the vent at the top and remove the lid. Press Cancel, then select Sauté. 4. Transfer the pork chops to a plate. Remove 1 tablespoon of cooking liquid from the pot and put in a small bowl with the cornstarch. Whisk well then return the mixture to the pot and whisk in the sour cream and butter until combined. Simmer to thicken, 4 to 5 minutes. Season with more salt and pepper if desired. Serve with mashed potatoes and steamed vegetables, and garnish with parsley.

Pork Cutlets with Aloha Salsa

Prep time: 20 minutes | Cook time: 7 to 9 minutes | Serves 4

Aloha Salsa:

1 cup fresh pineapple, chopped in small pieces

¼ cup red onion, finely chopped

¼ cup green or red bell pepper, chopped

½ teaspoon ground cinnamon

1 teaspoon low-sodium soy sauce

⅛ teaspoon crushed red pepper

⅛ teaspoon ground black pepper

2 eggs

2 tablespoons milk

¼ cup flour

¼ cup panko bread crumbs

4 teaspoons sesame seeds

1 pound (454 g) boneless, thin pork cutlets (⅜- to ½-inch thick)

lemon pepper and salt

¼ cup cornstarch

Oil for misting or cooking spray

1. In a medium bowl, stir together all ingredients for salsa. Cover and refrigerate while cooking pork. 2. Beat together eggs and milk in shallow dish. 3. In another shallow dish, mix together the flour, panko, and sesame seeds. 4. Sprinkle pork cutlets with lemon pepper and salt to taste. Most lemon pepper seasoning contains salt, so go easy adding extra. 5. Dip pork cutlets in cornstarch, egg mixture, and then panko coating. Spray both sides with oil or cooking spray. Place in the air fryer basket. 6. Close and lock the air fryer lid. Select Air Fry, set temperature to 390ºF (199ºC), and set time to 7 to 9 minutes. Press Start. Cook cutlets for 3 minutes. Turn cutlets over, spraying both sides, and continue cooking for 4 to 6 minutes or until well done. 7. Serve fried cutlets with salsa on the side.

Bone-in Pork Chops

Prep time: 5 minutes | Cook time: 10 to 12 minutes | Serves 2

1 pound (454 g) bone-in pork chops
1 tablespoon avocado oil
1 teaspoon smoked paprika

½ teaspoon onion powder
¼ teaspoon cayenne pepper
Sea salt and freshly ground black pepper, to taste

1. Brush the pork chops with the avocado oil. In a small dish, mix together the smoked paprika, onion powder, cayenne pepper, and salt and black pepper to taste. Sprinkle the seasonings over both sides of the pork chops. 2. Place the chops in the air fryer basket in a single layer, working in batches if necessary. Close and lock the air fryer lid. Select Air Fry, set temperature to 400ºF (204ºC), and set time to 10 to 12 minutes. Press Start. Cook until an instant-read thermometer reads 145ºF (63ºC) at the chops' thickest point. 3. Remove the chops from the basket and allow them to rest for 5 minutes before serving.

Sausage and Pork Meatballs

Prep time: 15 minutes | Cook time: 8 to 12 minutes | Serves 8

1 large egg
1 teaspoon gelatin
1 pound (454 g) ground pork
½ pound (227 g) Italian sausage, casings removed, crumbled
⅓ cup Parmesan cheese
¼ cup finely diced onion

1 tablespoon tomato paste
1 teaspoon minced garlic
1 teaspoon dried oregano
¼ teaspoon red pepper flakes
Sea salt and freshly ground black pepper, to taste
Keto-friendly marinara sauce, for serving

1. Beat the egg in a small bowl and sprinkle with the gelatin. Allow to sit for 5 minutes. 2. In a large bowl, combine the ground pork, sausage, Parmesan, onion, tomato paste, garlic, oregano, and red pepper flakes. Season with salt and black pepper. 3. Stir the gelatin mixture, then add it to the other ingredients and, using clean hands, mix to ensure that everything is well combined. Form into 1½-inch round meatballs. 4. Place the meatballs in the air fryer basket in a single layer, cooking in batches as needed. Close and lock the air fryer lid. Select Air Fry, set temperature to 400ºF (204ºC), and set time to 8 to 12 minutes. Press Start. Air fry for 5 minutes. Flip and cook for 3 to 7 minutes more, or until an instant-read thermometer reads 160ºF (71ºC).

Greek Lamb Rack

Prep time: 5 minutes | Cook time: 10 minutes | Serves 4

¼ cup freshly squeezed lemon juice
1 teaspoon oregano
2 teaspoons minced fresh rosemary
1 teaspoon minced fresh thyme

2 tablespoons minced garlic
Salt and freshly ground black pepper, to taste
2 to 4 tablespoons olive oil
1 lamb rib rack (7 to 8 ribs)

1. In a small mixing bowl, combine the lemon juice, oregano, rosemary, thyme, garlic, salt, pepper, and olive oil and mix well. 2. Rub the mixture over the lamb, covering all the meat. Put the rack of lamb in the air fryer basket. Close and lock the air fryer lid. Select Roast, set temperature to 360ºF (182ºC), and set time to 10 minutes. Press Start. Flip the rack halfway through. 3. After 10 minutes, measure the internal temperature of the rack of lamb reaches at least 145ºF (63ºC). 4. Serve immediately.

Onion Pork Kebabs

Prep time: 22 minutes | Cook time: 18 minutes | Serves 3

2 tablespoons tomato purée

½ fresh serrano, minced

⅓ teaspoon paprika

1 pound (454 g) pork, ground

½ cup green onions, finely chopped

3 cloves garlic, peeled and finely minced

1 teaspoon ground black pepper, or more to taste

1 teaspoon salt, or more to taste

1. Thoroughly combine all ingredients in a mixing dish. Then form your mixture into sausage shapes. 2. Place in air fryer basket. Close and lock the air fryer lid. Select Air Fry, set temperature to 355ºF (179ºC), and set time to 18 minutes. Press Start. 3. Mound salad on a serving platter, top with air-fried kebabs and serve warm. Bon appétit!

Lamb Keftedes

Prep time: 10 minutes | Cook time: 19 minutes | Serves 4

1 pound (454 g) ground lamb

2 large eggs

1 tablespoon peeled and finely diced cucumber

1 large carrot, scrubbed and grated

1 tablespoon chopped fresh mint leaves

1 tablespoon chopped fresh dill

1 teaspoon garlic powder

⅛ teaspoon ground cinnamon

1 tablespoon lemon zest

½ cup old-fashioned oats

3 tablespoons olive oil, divided

2 cups water

1. In a medium bowl, combine lamb, eggs, cucumber, carrot, mint, dill, garlic powder, cinnamon, lemon zest, and oats. Form mixture into twenty meatballs. Set aside. 2. Press the Sauté button on the pressure cooker and heat 2 tablespoons oil 30 seconds. Place ten meatballs around the edge of pot. Sear meatballs 4 minutes, making sure to get each side. Set aside. Add 1 tablespoon oil to pot and sear remaining meatballs 4 minutes. 3. Transfer seared meatballs to a 7-cup glass dish. 4. Discard extra juice and oil from the pressure cooker. Add water to pot. Insert steam rack. Place the glass dish on top of the steam rack. Close and lock the pressure cooker lid. 5. Press the Pressure Cook button and set time to 10 minutes at High pressure. Press Start. When pressure cooking is complete, let pressure release naturally for 10 minutes. Release any remaining pressure manually and then unlock lid. 6. Transfer meatballs to a serving dish and serve warm.

Chapter 9: Poultry

Sweet and Sour Chicken

Prep time: 10 minutes | Cook time: 7 minutes | Serves 6

1 cup apple cider vinegar

1 cup granulated sugar

½ cup ketchup

2 tablespoons soy sauce

1½ teaspoons garlic powder

1 teaspoon salt

1 cup cornstarch

2 pounds (907 g) boneless, skinless chicken breasts, cut into 1-inch chunks

½ teaspoon salt

¼ teaspoon black pepper

¼ cup vegetable oil

3 large eggs, beaten

1. In a small bowl, whisk together vinegar, sugar, ketchup, soy sauce, garlic powder, and salt. Set aside. 2. Pour cornstarch into a gallon-sized zip-top bag. 3. Season chicken with salt and pepper and place inside the bag of cornstarch. Close bag and shake until chicken is coated evenly. 4. Press Sauté button on pressure cooker. Pour in oil and let heat 1 minute. 5. Working in batches, remove chicken pieces from bag and dip into beaten eggs. 6. Shake to remove any excess egg, then layer chicken evenly in hot oil on the bottom of pot. Let cook, unmoved, for 30 seconds. 7. Flip and cook another 30 seconds. 8. Remove from pot and continue with remaining chicken. 9. Once chicken is cooked and removed from pressure cooker, pour sauce into pot and deglaze the pot. 10. Add chicken and turn to coat with sauce. 11. Close and lock the pressure cooker lid and set pressure release to Sealing. 12. Press Pressure Cook button and set time to 3 minutes at High pressure. Press Start. 13. When pressure cooking is complete, allow pressure to release naturally and then unlock lid and remove it. Serve warm.

Turkey with Berry Compote

Prep time: 15 minutes | Cook time: 45 minutes | Serves 12

1 teaspoon salt

½ teaspoon garlic powder

½ teaspoon dried thyme

½ teaspoon pepper

2 boneless skinless turkey breast halves (2 pounds / 907 g each)

⅓ cup water

Compote:

2 medium apples, peeled and finely chopped

2 cups fresh raspberries

2 cups fresh blueberries

1 cup white grape juice

¼ teaspoon crushed red pepper flakes

¼ teaspoon ground ginger

1. Mix salt, garlic powder, thyme and pepper; rub over turkey breasts. Place in pressure cooker. Pour water around turkey. Close and lock the pressure cooker lid; make sure vent is closed. Select Pressure Cook and set time to 30 minutes at High pressure. Press Start. When pressure cooking is complete, allow pressure to naturally release for 10 minutes, then use a quick release. A thermometer inserted in turkey breasts should read at least 165°F (74°C). 2. Carefully remove turkey and cooking juices from pressure cooker; tent with foil. Let stand before slicing while you prepare the compote. 3. In pressure cooker, select Sauté. Add compote ingredients. Bring to a boil. Reduce the heat; cook, uncovered, stirring occasionally, until slightly thickened and apples are tender, 15 to 20 minutes. Serve turkey with compote.

Pulled Chicken Sandwiches

Prep time: 10 minutes | Cook time: 15 minutes | Serves 4

1 pound (454 g) boneless, skinless chicken breasts
¼ teaspoon salt
⅛ teaspoon black pepper

1½ cups barbecue sauce, divided
1 cup water
4 hamburger buns

1. Place chicken in a 6-cup metal bowl. Season chicken with salt and pepper and brush with 1 cup barbecue sauce. 2. Pour water in pressure cooker. Add steam rack to pressure cooker. 3. Create a foil sling and carefully lower bowl of chicken into pressure cooker. 4. Close and lock the pressure cooker lid and set pressure release to Sealing. 5. Press Pressure Cook button and set time to 15 minutes at High pressure. Press Start. 6. When pressure cooking is complete, allow pressure to release naturally for 10 minutes, then release the remaining pressure manually. Unlock lid and remove it. 7. Use foil sling to remove the bowl of chicken. 8. Drain any water in bowl and shred chicken with two forks. 9. Add remaining ½ cup barbecue sauce and stir to combine. 10. Serve pulled chicken on warmed hamburger buns.

Juicy Paprika Chicken Breast

Prep time: 5 minutes | Cook time: 30 minutes | Serves 4

Oil, for spraying
4 (6-ounce / 170-g) boneless, skinless chicken breasts
1 tablespoon olive oil
1 tablespoon paprika

1 tablespoon packed light brown sugar
½ teaspoon cayenne pepper
½ teaspoon onion powder
½ teaspoon granulated garlic

1. Line the air fryer basket with parchment and spray lightly with oil. 2. Brush the chicken with the olive oil. 3. In a small bowl, mix together the paprika, brown sugar, cayenne pepper, onion powder, and garlic and sprinkle it over the chicken. 4. Place the chicken in the prepared basket. You may need to work in batches, depending on the size of your basket. 5. Close and lock the air fryer lid. Select Air Fry, set temperature to 360ºF (182ºC), and set time to 30 minutes. Press Start. Air fry for 15 minutes, flip, and cook for another 15 minutes, or until the internal temperature reaches 165ºF (74ºC). Serve immediately.

Honey-Sriracha Chicken

Prep time: 10 minutes | Cook time: 12 minutes | Serves 4

4 chicken breasts, diced
5 tablespoons soy sauce
2 to 3 tablespoons honey
¼ cup sugar

4 tablespoons cold water
1 tablespoon minced garlic
2 to 3 tablespoons Sriracha
2 tablespoons cornstarch

1. In the pressure cooker, whisk together soy sauce, honey, sugar, 2 tablespoons of water, garlic, and Sriracha until combined. 2. Toss the chicken breasts in the mixture. Close and lock the pressure cooker lid. 3. Select Pressure Cook and set time to 9 minutes at High pressure. Press Start. 4. Meanwhile, in a small bowl combine 2 tablespoons of water and cornstarch. 5. When pressure cooking is complete, use a quick release. Carefully unlock the lid. 6. Pour the cornstarch mixture into the pot. 7. Select Sauté, simmer and stir occasionally until the sauce begins to thicken. 8. Serve.

Cajun Chicken Bowls

Prep time: 5 minutes | Cook time: 11 minutes | Serves 4

1¼ cups uncooked long-grain white rice, rinsed
1¼ cups chicken stock
5 teaspoons Cajun seasoning

2 pounds (907 g) boneless, skinless chicken breast, cut into bite-size pieces
1 red bell pepper, seeded and chopped

1. Press Sauté to preheat the pressure cooker. Once hot, add the rice. Toast the rice in the dry pot, stirring frequently, about 2 minutes. 2. Add the chicken stock, Cajun seasoning, chicken and bell pepper and stir. 3. Close and lock the pressure cooker lid. Select Pressure Cook and set time to 9 minutes at High pressure. Press Start. 4. When pressure cooking is complete, use a quick release and carefully remove the lid. Season to taste and serve.

Brazilian Tempero Baiano Chicken Drumsticks

Prep time: 30 minutes | Cook time: 20 minutes | Serves 4

1 teaspoon cumin seeds
1 teaspoon dried oregano
1 teaspoon dried parsley
1 teaspoon ground turmeric
½ teaspoon coriander seeds
1 teaspoon kosher salt

½ teaspoon black peppercorns
½ teaspoon cayenne pepper
¼ cup fresh lime juice
2 tablespoons olive oil
1½ pounds (680 g) chicken drumsticks

1. In a clean coffee grinder or spice mill, combine the cumin, oregano, parsley, turmeric, coriander seeds, salt, peppercorns, and cayenne. Process until finely ground. 2. In a small bowl, combine the ground spices with the lime juice and oil. Place the chicken in a resealable plastic bag. Add the marinade, seal, and massage until the chicken is well coated. Marinate at room temperature for 30 minutes or in the refrigerator for up to 24 hours. 3. When you are ready to cook, place the drumsticks skin side up in the air fryer basket. Close and lock the air fryer lid. Select Roast, set temperature to 400°F (204°C), and set time to 20 to 25 minutes. Press Start. Turn the drumsticks halfway through the cooking time. Use a meat thermometer to ensure that the chicken has reached an internal temperature of 165°F (74°C). 4. Serve with plenty of napkins.

Blackened Cajun Chicken Tenders

Prep time: 10 minutes | Cook time: 17 minutes | Serves 4

2 teaspoons paprika
1 teaspoon chili powder
½ teaspoon garlic powder
½ teaspoon dried thyme
¼ teaspoon onion powder

⅛ teaspoon ground cayenne pepper
2 tablespoons coconut oil
1 pound (454 g) boneless, skinless chicken tenders
¼ cup full-fat ranch dressing

1. In a small bowl, combine all seasonings. 2. Drizzle oil over chicken tenders and then generously coat each tender in the spice mixture. Place tenders into the air fryer basket. 3. Close and lock the air fryer lid. Select Air Fry, set temperature to 375°F (191°C), and set time to 17 minutes. Press Start. 4. Tenders will be 165°F (74°C) internally when fully cooked. Serve with ranch dressing for dipping.

Thanksgiving Turkey Breast

Prep time: 5 minutes | Cook time: 30 minutes | Serves 4

1½ teaspoons fine sea salt
1 teaspoon ground black pepper
1 teaspoon chopped fresh rosemary leaves
1 teaspoon chopped fresh sage
1 teaspoon chopped fresh tarragon

1 teaspoon chopped fresh thyme leaves
1 (2-pound / 907-g) turkey breast
3 tablespoons ghee or unsalted butter, melted
3 tablespoons Dijon mustard

1. Spray the air fryer basket with avocado oil. 2. In a small bowl, stir together the salt, pepper, and herbs until well combined. Season the turkey breast generously on all sides with the seasoning. 3. In another small bowl, stir together the ghee and Dijon. Brush the ghee mixture on all sides of the turkey breast. 4. Place the turkey breast in the air fryer basket. Close and lock the air fryer lid. Select Air Fry, set temperature to 390ºF (199ºC), and set time to 30 minutes. Press Start. Cook until the internal temperature reaches 165ºF (74ºC). Transfer the breast to a cutting board and allow it to rest for 10 minutes before cutting it into ½-inch-thick slices. 5. Store leftovers in an airtight container in the refrigerator for up to 4 days or in the freezer for up to a month.

Celery Chicken

Prep time: 10 minutes | Cook time: 15 minutes | Serves 4

½ cup soy sauce
2 tablespoons hoisin sauce
4 teaspoons minced garlic
1 teaspoon freshly ground black pepper

8 boneless, skinless chicken tenderloins
1 cup chopped celery
1 medium red bell pepper, diced
Olive oil spray

1. Spray the air fryer basket lightly with olive oil spray. 2. In a large bowl, mix together the soy sauce, hoisin sauce, garlic, and black pepper to make a marinade. Add the chicken, celery, and bell pepper and toss to coat. 3. Shake the excess marinade off the chicken, place it and the vegetables in the air fryer basket, and lightly spray with olive oil spray. You may need to cook them in batches. Reserve the remaining marinade. 4. Close and lock the air fryer lid. Select Air Fry, set temperature to 375ºF (191ºC), and set time to 15 minutes. Press Start. Air fry for 8 minutes. Turn the chicken over and brush with some of the remaining marinade. Air fry for an additional 5 to 7 minutes, or until the chicken reaches an internal temperature of at least 165ºF (74ºC). Serve.

Barbecue Chicken

Prep time: 10 minutes | Cook time: 18 to 20 minutes | Serves 4

⅓ cup no-salt-added tomato sauce
2 tablespoons low-sodium grainy mustard
2 tablespoons apple cider vinegar
1 tablespoon honey
2 garlic cloves, minced

1 jalapeño pepper, minced
3 tablespoons minced onion
4 (5-ounce / 142-g) low-sodium boneless, skinless chicken breasts

1. In a small bowl, stir together the tomato sauce, mustard, cider vinegar, honey, garlic, jalapeño, and onion. 2. Brush the chicken breasts with some sauce and place in air fryer basket. Close and lock the air fryer lid. Select Air Fry, set temperature to 370ºF (188ºC), and set time to 18 to 20 minutes. Press Start. 3. Air fry for 10 minutes. Remove the air fryer basket and turn the chicken; brush with more sauce. Air fry for 5 minutes more. 4. Remove the air fryer basket and turn the chicken again; brush with more sauce. Air fry for 3 to 5 minutes more, or until the chicken reaches an internal temperature of 165ºF (74ºC) on a meat thermometer. Discard any remaining sauce. Serve immediately.

Chicken Legs with Leeks

Prep time: 30 minutes | Cook time: 18 minutes | Serves 6

2 leeks, sliced
2 large-sized tomatoes, chopped
3 cloves garlic, minced
½ teaspoon dried oregano

6 chicken legs, boneless and skinless
½ teaspoon smoked cayenne pepper
2 tablespoons olive oil
A freshly ground nutmeg

1. In a mixing dish, thoroughly combine all ingredients, minus the leeks. Place in the refrigerator and let it marinate overnight. 2. Lay the leeks onto the bottom of the air fryer basket. Top with the chicken legs. Close and lock the air fryer lid. Select Roast, set temperature to 375ºF (191ºC), and set time to 18 minutes. Press Start. Turn halfway through. Serve with hoisin sauce.

Chapter 10: Fish and Seafood

Salmon Cakes

Prep time: 15 minutes | Cook time: 9 minutes | Serves 4

½ pound (227 g) cooked salmon, shredded
2 large eggs
2 medium green onions, sliced
1 cup bread crumbs
½ cup flat leaf parsley, chopped
¼ cup soy sauce

1 tablespoon Worcestershire sauce
½ tablespoon garlic powder
1 teaspoon salt
½ teaspoon cayenne pepper
¼ teaspoon celery seed
4 tablespoons olive oil

1. In a large bowl, combine salmon, eggs, green onions, bread crumbs, parsley, soy sauce, Worcestershire, garlic powder, salt, cayenne, and celery seed. Mix together with clean hands until combined. 2. Press Sauté button on pressure cooker and add oil. 3. Take golf ball-sized clumps of salmon mixture. Roll into balls and then flatten to form a cake. Place salmon cakes in an even layer in pressure cooker. 4. Let cook 2 minutes until golden brown. Flip and cook an additional 2 minutes. 5. Repeat with remaining salmon mixture. 6. Store salmon cakes under foil until ready to serve.

Tiger Prawns Paella

Prep time: 10 minutes | Cook time: 13 minutes | Serves 2 to 4

1 cup tiger prawns, peeled and deveined
1 tablespoon olive oil
1 small red onion, roughly chopped
1 red bell pepper, chopped
2 chorizo sausage slices
¾ cup risotto rice or paella rice
2 cups vegetable stock (or chicken stock)

¾ cup green peas, frozen
1 cup sweet corn
1 tablespoon fresh parsley, finely chopped
1 teaspoon salt
A pinch of saffron threads
1 whole lemon, quartered

1. Preheat the pressure cooker by selecting Sauté. Add and heat the oil. 2. Add the onion and chorizo slices. Stir and sauté for 3 minute. 3. Add the tiger prawns and cook for 2 to 3 minutes more, stirring occasionally. 4. Add the rice and stock. Stir well. 5. Add the peas, sweet corn, and parsley. Season with salt and saffron. 6. Close and lock the pressure cooker lid. Select Pressure Cook and set time to 7 minutes at High pressure. Press Start. 7. When pressure cooking is complete, use a quick release. Unlock and carefully open the lid. 8. Place the lemon on top. Close and lock the pressure cooker lid and let sit for 10 minutes. Serve.

Lobster Tails

Prep time: 5 minutes | Cook time: 5 minutes | Serves 4

4 lobster tails, cut in half
1 cup water

½ cup white wine
½ cup butter, melted

1. Pour the water and wine into the pressure cooker and insert a steam rack. 2. Place the lobster tails on the rack. 3. Select Pressure Cook and set time to 5 minutes at Low pressure. Press Start. 4. When pressure cooking is complete, use a natural release for 10 minutes, and then release any remaining pressure manually. Open the lid. 5. Transfer the legs to a serving bowl. 6. Add melted butter and serve.

Apple Cider Mussels

Prep time: 10 minutes | Cook time: 2 minutes | Serves 5

2 pounds (907 g) mussels, cleaned, peeled
1 teaspoon onion powder
1 teaspoon ground cumin

1 tablespoon avocado oil
¼ cup apple cider vinegar

1. Mix mussels with onion powder, ground cumin, avocado oil, and apple cider vinegar. 2. Put the mussels in the air fryer basket. Close and lock the air fryer lid. Select Air Fry, set temperature to 395ºF (202ºC), and set time to 2 minutes. Press Start.

Buffalo Shrimp Mac and Cheese

Prep time: 15 minutes | Cook time: 10 minutes | Serves 6

2 cups 2% milk
1 cup half-and-half cream
1 tablespoon unsalted butter
1 teaspoon ground mustard
½ teaspoon onion powder
¼ teaspoon white pepper
¼ teaspoon ground nutmeg
1½ cups uncooked elbow macaroni

2 cups shredded Cheddar cheese
1 cup shredded Gouda or Swiss cheese
¾ pound (340 g) frozen cooked salad shrimp, thawed
1 cup crumbled blue cheese
2 tablespoons Louisiana-style hot sauce
2 tablespoons minced fresh chives
2 tablespoons minced fresh parsley
Additional Louisiana-style hot sauce, optional

1. In pressure cooker, combine the first seven ingredients; stir in macaroni. Close and lock the pressure cooker lid; make sure vent is closed. Select Pressure Cook and set time to 3 minutes at High pressure. Press Start. When pressure cooking is complete, allow pressure to naturally release for 4 minutes, then use a quick release. 2. Select Sauté. Stir in shredded cheeses, shrimp, blue cheese and hot sauce. Cook until heated through, 5 to 6 minutes. Just before serving, stir in chives, parsley and, if desired, additional hot sauce.

Fish Curry

Prep time: 15 minutes | Cook time: 10 minutes | Serves 4

1½ pounds (680 g) fish fillets, cut into 2-inch pieces
2 tablespoons olive oil
4 cloves garlic, minced
2 medium onions, chopped
2 teaspoons fresh ginger, grated finely
½ teaspoon ground turmeric
1 teaspoon red chili powder
2 teaspoons ground cumin

2 teaspoons ground coriander
2 tablespoons curry powder
2 cups unsweetened coconut milk
1 cup tomatoes, chopped
2 Serrano peppers, seeded and chopped
Salt, to taste
1 tablespoon fresh lemon juice

1. Select Sauté on the pressure cooker and heat the oil. 2. Add the garlic, onion, and ginger and sauté for 4 minutes. 3. Add the turmeric, chili powder, cumin, coriander, and curry. Stir and cook for 1 minute more. 4. Pour in the coconut milk and stir well. 5. Add the fish, tomatoes, and Serrano pepper, stir. Season with salt. 6. Press the Cancel button to stop the Sauté function. 7. Close and lock the pressure cooker lid. Select Pressure Cook and set time to 5 minutes at Low pressure. Press Start. 8. When pressure cooking is complete, use a natural release for 10 minutes, then release any remaining pressure manually. Open the lid. 9. Drizzle the dish with the lemon juice and serve.

Salmon with Cauliflower

Prep time: 10 minutes | Cook time: 25 minutes | Serves 4

1 pound (454 g) salmon fillet, diced
1 cup shredded cauliflower
1 tablespoon dried cilantro

1 tablespoon coconut oil, melted
1 teaspoon ground turmeric
¼ cup coconut cream

1. Mix salmon with cauliflower, dried cilantro, ground turmeric, coconut cream, and coconut oil. 2. Transfer the salmon mixture into the air fryer basket. Close and lock the air fryer lid. Select Bake, set temperature to 350ºF (177ºC), and set time to 25 minutes. Press Start. Stir the meal every 5 minutes to avoid the burning.

Chili Lime Shrimp

Prep time: 5 minutes | Cook time: 5 minutes | Serves 4

1 pound (454 g) medium shrimp, peeled and deveined
1 tablespoon salted butter, melted
2 teaspoons chili powder
¼ teaspoon garlic powder

¼ teaspoon salt
¼ teaspoon ground black pepper
½ small lime, zested and juiced, divided

1. In a medium bowl, toss shrimp with butter, then sprinkle with chili powder, garlic powder, salt, pepper, and lime zest. 2. Place shrimp into ungreased air fryer basket. Close and lock the air fryer lid. Select Air Fry, set temperature to 400ºF (204ºC), and set time to 5 minutes. Press Start. Shrimp will be firm and form a "C" shape when done. 3. Transfer shrimp to a large serving dish and drizzle with lime juice. Serve warm.

Oregano Tilapia Fingers

Prep time: 15 minutes | Cook time: 9 minutes | Serves 4

1 pound (454 g) tilapia fillet
½ cup coconut flour
2 eggs, beaten
½ teaspoon ground paprika
1 teaspoon dried oregano
1 teaspoon avocado oil

1. Cut the tilapia fillets into fingers and sprinkle with ground paprika and dried oregano. 2. Then dip the tilapia fingers in eggs and coat in the coconut flour. 3. Sprinkle fish fingers with avocado oil and place in air fryer basket. Close and lock the air fryer lid. Select Air Fry, set temperature to 370ºF (188ºC), and set time to 9 minutes. Press Start.

Sweet Tilapia Fillets

Prep time: 5 minutes | Cook time: 14 minutes | Serves 4

2 tablespoons erythritol
1 tablespoon apple cider vinegar

4 tilapia fillets, boneless
1 teaspoon olive oil

1. Mix apple cider vinegar with olive oil and erythritol. 2. Then rub the tilapia fillets with the sweet mixture and put in the air fryer basket in one layer. Close and lock the air fryer lid. Select Air Fry, set temperature to 360°F (182°C), and set time to 14 minutes. Press Start. Flip halfway through.

Marinated Swordfish Skewers

Prep time: 30 minutes | Cook time: 6 to 8 minutes | Serves 4

1 pound (454 g) filleted swordfish
¼ cup avocado oil
2 tablespoons freshly squeezed lemon juice
1 tablespoon minced fresh parsley

2 teaspoons Dijon mustard
Sea salt and freshly ground black pepper, to taste
3 ounces (85 g) cherry tomatoes

1. Cut the fish into 1½-inch chunks, picking out any remaining bones. 2. In a large bowl, whisk together the oil, lemon juice, parsley, and Dijon mustard. Season to taste with salt and pepper. Add the fish and toss to coat the pieces. Cover and marinate the fish chunks in the refrigerator for 30 minutes. 3. Remove the fish from the marinade. Thread the fish and cherry tomatoes on 4 skewers, alternating as you go. 4. Place the skewers in the air fryer basket. Close and lock the air fryer lid. Select Air Fry, set temperature to 400°F (204°C), and set time to 6 to 8 minutes. Press Start. Air fry for 3 minutes. Flip the skewers and cook for 3 to 5 minutes longer, until the fish is cooked through and an instant-read thermometer reads 140°F (60°C).

Chapter 11: Desserts

Chai-Spiced Rice Pudding

Prep time: 10 minutes | Cook time: 5 minutes | Serves 4

1 cup uncooked Arborio rice
1½ cups water
Pinch of salt
2 cups whole milk or almond milk, divided
½ cup sugar
2 large eggs
½ teaspoon pure vanilla extract

½ teaspoon ground cardamom
½ teaspoon ground allspice
2 teaspoons ground cinnamon
¼ teaspoon ground cloves
1 tablespoon ground ginger
½ cup golden raisins

1. In the pressure cooker, combine the rice, water and salt. Stir well. 2. Close and lock the pressure cooker lid. Select Pressure Cook and set time to 3 minutes at High pressure. Press Start. 3. Allow the pressure to naturally release for 10 minutes. After 10 minutes, quick release any remaining pressure. 4. Remove the lid. Add ½ cup of the milk and the sugar. Stir to combine. 5. In a small bowl, mix together the eggs and the remaining 1½ cups of milk along with the vanilla, cardamom, allspice, cinnamon, cloves, ginger and raisins. 6. Press Sauté. Pour the egg through a mesh strainer into the pressure cooker. Stir to combine. 7. Once the pudding starts to simmer, press Cancel. Stir in the raisins. 8. The pudding can be served warm or cooled completely in the refrigerator.

Protein Powder Doughnut Holes

Prep time: 25 minutes | Cook time: 6 minutes | Makes 12 holes

½ cup blanched finely ground almond flour
½ cup low-carb vanilla protein powder
½ cup granular erythritol
½ teaspoon baking powder

1 large egg
5 tablespoons unsalted butter, melted
½ teaspoon vanilla extract

1. Mix all ingredients in a large bowl. Place into the freezer for 20 minutes. 2. Wet your hands with water and roll the dough into twelve balls. 3. Cut a piece of parchment to fit your air fryer basket. Working in batches as necessary, place doughnut holes into the air fryer basket on top of parchment. 4. Close and lock the air fryer lid. Select Air Fry, set temperature to 380ºF (193ºC), and set time to 6 minutes. Press Start. 5. Flip doughnut holes halfway through the cooking time. 6. Let cool completely before serving.

Easy Chocolate Donuts

Prep time: 5 minutes | Cook time: 8 minutes | Serves 8

1 (8-ounce / 227-g) can jumbo biscuits
Cooking oil

Chocolate sauce, for drizzling

1. Separate the biscuit dough into 8 biscuits and place them on a flat work surface. Use a small circle cookie cutter or a biscuit cutter to cut a hole in the center of each biscuit. You can also cut the holes using a knife. 2. Spray the air fryer basket with cooking oil. 3. Put 4 donuts in the basket. Do not stack. Spray with cooking oil. Close and lock the air fryer lid. Select Air Fry, set temperature to 375ºF (191ºC), and set time to 8 minutes. Press Start. Air fry for 4 minutes. Flip the donuts and air fry for an additional 4 minutes. 4. Remove the cooked donuts from the basket, then repeat steps for the remaining 4 donuts. 5. Drizzle chocolate sauce over the donuts and enjoy while warm.

Fruit Compote

Prep time: 8 minutes | Cook time: 15 minutes | Serves 6

1 cup apple juice

1 cup dry white wine

2 tablespoons granulated sugar

1 cinnamon stick

¼ teaspoon ground nutmeg

Zest of 1 medium lemon

Zest of 1 medium orange

3 medium Granny Smith apples, peeled, cored, and chopped

3 medium Bartlett pears, peeled, cored, and chopped

½ cup dried cherries, cranberries, or raisins

1. In the pressure cooker, combine the apple juice and wine and press the Sauté button. Bring to a boil and stir in the sugar until dissolved, about 3 minutes. Add the cinnamon stick, nutmeg, lemon zest, and orange zest. Adjust to Low and simmer 5 minutes. 2. Add the apples and pears to the pot and stir to mix ingredients. Close and lock the pressure cooker lid, select Pressure Cook and set time to 3 minutes at High pressure. Press Start. When pressure cooking is complete, use a quick release and then unlock lid. 3. Use a slotted spoon to transfer the cooked fruit to a serving bowl. Press the Sauté button on the pot to bring juices to a boil; boil and stir until reduced to a syrup that will coat the back of a spoon. 4. Stir the dried cherries, cranberries, or raisins in with the cooked fruit in the bowl and pour the syrup over the fruit mixture. Stir to mix. Allow to cool slightly, then cover with plastic wrap and chill overnight in the refrigerator.

Cinnamon-Sugar Almonds

Prep time: 5 minutes | Cook time: 8 minutes | Serves 4

1 cup whole almonds

2 tablespoons salted butter, melted

1 tablespoon sugar

½ teaspoon ground cinnamon

1. In a medium bowl, combine the almonds, butter, sugar, and cinnamon. Mix well to ensure all the almonds are coated with the spiced butter. 2. Transfer the almonds to the air fryer basket and shake so they are in a single layer. Close and lock the air fryer lid. Select Air Fry, set temperature to 300°F (149°C), and set time to 8 minutes. Press Start. Stir the almonds halfway through the cooking time. 3. Let cool completely before serving.

Stout-Poached Pears

Prep time: 5 minutes | Cook time: 9 minutes | Serves 2

3 peeled (stem on) firm Bartlett pears

1½ cups (1 bottle) stout beer

1 vanilla bean, split lengthwise and seeds scraped

½ cup packed brown sugar

1. Slice a thin layer from the bottom of each pear so they can stand upright. Using a melon baller, scoop out the seeds and core from the bottom. 2. In the pressure cooker, stir together the beer, vanilla bean and seeds, and brown sugar. Place the pears upright in the pot. 3. Close and lock the pressure cooker lid. Select Pressure Cook and set time to 9 minutes at High pressure. Press Start. Quick release the pressure in the pot and remove the lid. Press Cancel. 4. Using tongs, carefully remove the pears by their stems and transfer to a plate. Set aside. Select Sauté and simmer the liquid in the pot until reduced by half. 5. Strain the liquid into a bowl through a fine-mesh sieve, then pour over the pears. Serve at room temperature or chilled, plain or with whipped cream and a drizzle of chocolate sauce.

Spiced Oat-Stuffed Apples

Prep time: 5 minutes | Cook time: 45 minutes | Serves 4

1 cup rolled oats
¼ cup maple syrup
1 tablespoon ground flaxseed
1 tablespoon spiced rum (or 1 teaspoon pure vanilla extract)

1 teaspoon ground cinnamon
Pinch of ground cloves
Pinch of salt
4 medium apples, cored and cut in half vertically

1. Mix the oats, maple syrup, flaxseed, spiced rum, cinnamon, cloves and salt in a bowl. 2. Place a steam rack in your pressure cooker and pour in 1½ cups water. 3. Using about 2 tablespoons of the filling, cover the cut side of the apple and press the mixture down into the cavity. Place in a pan that fits in your pressure cooker. Repeat with each apple half. Cover the dish with foil and place in the pressure cooker. 4. Select Pressure Cook and set time to 30 minutes at High pressure. Press Start. Let the pressure release naturally. If your apples aren't easily pierced with a fork, put the lid back on and cook for another 15 to 25 minutes.

Apple Crumble Cobbler

Prep time: 10 minutes | Cook time: 2 minutes | Serves 4

5 Granny Smith apples, cored, peeled, and cut into 1-inch cubes
2 teaspoons ground cinnamon
½ teaspoon ground nutmeg
2 tablespoons maple syrup
2 tablespoons caramel syrup, plus more for topping
½ cup water

4 tablespoons (½ stick) salted butter
⅓ cup light-brown sugar
¾ cup old-fashioned oats (not instant)
¼ cup all-purpose flour
½ teaspoon sea salt
Vanilla ice cream, for serving

1. Place the apples in the pressure cooker and top with the cinnamon, nutmeg, maple syrup, caramel syrup, and water. Stir together well until a liquid consistency is reached and the apples are coated. 2. Create the topping: In a microwave-safe bowl, melt the butter, then add the brown sugar, oats, flour, and salt. Mix well and pour over the apple mixture in the pot. 3. Close and lock the pressure cooker lid, move the valve to the sealing position, and select Pressure Cook and set time to 2 minutes at High pressure. Press Start. When done, allow a full natural release (this will take 20 to 30 minutes). 4. Serve right out of the pot, topped with vanilla ice cream and some more caramel sauce, if desired.

Poached Pears with Spiced Pomegranate Sauce

Prep time: 5 minutes | Cook time: 12 minutes | Serves 4

4 pears, peeled
½ cup pomegranate juice
½ cup orange juice
¼ cup pomegranate seeds

2 star anise pods
1 teaspoon fresh grated ginger
½ teaspoon ground cinnamon
¼ cup coconut sugar

1. Into the pressure cooker, add all the ingredients, except for the pears. Use a whisk or a spoon to mix until the sugar is mostly dissolved. 2. Place the steam rack into the cooker and place the pears on top. 3. Close and lock the pressure cooker lid, select Pressure Cook and set time to 7 minutes at High pressure. Press Start. 4. Use the quick release method to release the steam from the cooker. 5. Let the cooker sit for 7 to 10 minutes before removing the lid. 6. Carefully open the lid and remove the pears from the cooker. Set aside. 7. Turn the setting on the cooker to Sauté. 8. Cook the sauce, stirring frequently, for approximately 5 minutes, or until it reduces and thickens. 9. Place the pears on serving plates and drizzle the pomegranate sauce over the top before serving.

Cream Cheese Shortbread Cookies

Prep time: 30 minutes | Cook time: 20 minutes | Makes 12 cookies

¼ cup coconut oil, melted
2 ounces (57 g) cream cheese, softened
½ cup granular erythritol

1 large egg, whisked
2 cups blanched finely ground almond flour
1 teaspoon almond extract

1. Combine all ingredients in a large bowl to form a firm ball. 2. Place dough on a sheet of plastic wrap and roll into a 12-inch-long log shape. Roll log in plastic wrap and place in refrigerator 30 minutes to chill. 3. Remove log from plastic and slice into twelve equal cookies. Cut two sheets of parchment paper to fit air fryer basket. Place six cookies on each ungreased sheet. Place one sheet with cookies into air fryer basket. Close and lock the air fryer lid. Select Bake, set temperature to 320ºF (160ºC), and set time to 10 minutes. Press Start. Turn cookies halfway through cooking. They will be lightly golden when done. Repeat with remaining cookies. 4. Let cool 15 minutes before serving to avoid crumbling.

Chapter 12: Dehydrate

Dehydrated Strawberries

Prep time: 10 minutes | Cook time: 2 hours | Serves 4

1 pound (454 g) fresh strawberries

1. Line the dehydrator tray with parchment paper. 2. Wash strawberries and cut off stem ends. Cut strawberries into slices, about ⅛ inch thick. 3. Place the sliced strawberries on the dehydrator tray. Space them so the pieces are not touching. 4. Close and lock the air fryer lid. Select Dehydrate, set temperature to 170°F (77°C), and set time to 2 hours. Press Start. 5. Cook for 30 minutes. Use tongs to turn the berries. 6. Cook for another 30 minutes. Repeat this until strawberry slices are leathery. 7. Allow the slices to cool completely. Transfer dried strawberry slices to an airtight container. They will keep up to 5 days.

Tasty Salmon Jerky

Prep time: 20 minutes | Cook time: 3 hours | Serves 10

1¾ pounds (794 g) fillet wild Alaskan salmon, skin on, bones removed

½ cup low-sodium soy sauce

1 tablespoon lemon juice

1 tablespoon brown sugar

2 teaspoons mixed whole peppercorns

1 teaspoon lemon zest

½ teaspoon liquid smoke

½ teaspoon celery seeds

½ teaspoon onion powder

½ teaspoon garlic powder

¼ teaspoon kosher salt

1. Freeze salmon for 1 hour. 2. In the meantime, in a large bowl, combine the soy sauce, lemon juice, sugar, peppercorns, lemon zest, liquid smoke, celery seeds, onion and garlic powders, and salt. 3. Remove the salmon from the freezer and cut it into thin strips (about ½ inch), then place in the marinade. Cover and marinate for 1 to 3 hours in the fridge. 4. Remove strips and place on a plate, patting dry with a paper towel. 5. Place the salmon strips on the dehydrator tray in a single layer. Close and lock the air fryer lid. Select Dehydrate, set temperature to 170°F (77°C), and set time to 3 hours. Press Start. Flip over halfway through. Salmon is done when dried all the way through, but slightly chewy. 6. Store in a cool dry place in a sealed container.

Homemade Beef Jerky

Prep time: 10 minutes | Cook time: 3 to 4 hours | Serves 8

12 ounces (340 g) top sirloin beef

1 garlic clove, minced

1 inch piece fresh gingerroot, peeled and grated

2 tablespoons reduced sodium soy sauce

1 tablespoon turbinado sugar

1 tablespoon chili paste (such as Sambal Oelek)

1 tablespoon rice vinegar

1. Using a sharp knife, thinly slice beef and place in a resealable bag. 2. In a bowl, combine garlic, ginger, soy sauce, sugar chili paste and rice vinegar; whisk well. 3. Pour marinade into bag, seal and place in the refrigerator for at least 4 or up to 24 hours. 4. When ready to cook, remove pieces of beef from a marinade and pat dry with a paper towel. 5. Place the beef on the dehydrator tray. Close and lock the air fryer lid. Select Dehydrate, set temperature to 160°F (71°C), and set time to 3 to 4 hours. Press Start. 6. Checking the jerky periodically for desired doneness. Allow to cool completely and then store in an airtight container.

Candied Bacon

Prep time: 10 minutes | Cook time: 4 hours | Makes 6 slices

6 slices bacon
3 tablespoons light brown sugar
2 tablespoons rice vinegar

2 tablespoons chilli paste
1 tablespoon soy sauce

1. Mix brown sugar, rice vinegar, chilli paste, and soy sauce in a bowl. 2. Add bacon slices and mix until the slices are evenly coated. 3. Marinate for up to 3 hours or until ready to dehydrate. 4. Discard the marinade, then place the bacon on the dehydrator tray. Close and lock the air fryer lid. Select Dehydrate, set temperature to 170ºF (77ºC), and set time to 4 hours. Press Start. 5. Remove from the tray when done and let the bacon cool down for 5 minutes, then serve.

Dried Mushrooms

Prep time: 30 minutes | Cook time: 4 hours | Makes 2½ quarts

4 to 5 pounds (1.8 to 2.3 kg) fresh mushrooms, washed, rinsed and drained well.

1. Rinse whole mushrooms well under cold running water. Gently scrub any visible dirt away with out damaging the mushroom. Pat dry with paper towels if needed. 2. Break the stem off of each mushroom and slice into ¼ to ½ inch thick slices with a sharp knife. 3. Place the sliced mushrooms on the parchment-lined dehydrator tray. Close and lock the air fryer lid. Select Dehydrate, set temperature to 170ºF (77ºC), and set time to 4 hours. Press Start. 4. Check the mushrooms after 1 hour and flip them over for even drying. Check the mushroom slices every hour. 5. As the mushroom slices dry, remove them from the tray and allow to cool on the racks or a paper towel. 6. Store dried mushroom slices in an airtight glass container.

Cinnamon Oranges

Prep time: 10 minutes | Cook time: 6 hours | Serves 3

2 large oranges, cut into ⅛-inch-thick slices
½ teaspoon ground star anise

½ teaspoon ground cinnamon
1 tablespoon chocolate hazelnut spread (optional)

1. Sprinkle spices on the orange slices. 2. Place the orange slices on the dehydrator tray. Close and lock the air fryer lid. Select Dehydrate, set temperature to 140ºF (60ºC), and set time to 6 hours. Press Start. 3. Remove when done, and if desired serve with chocolate hazelnut spread.

Dehydrated Cinnamon Pineapple

Prep time: 10 minutes | Cook time: 12 hours | Serves 6

1 pineapple, peeled, cored and sliced ¼ inch thick
1 tablespoon coconut palm sugar
2 teaspoons ground cinnamon

½ teaspoon ground ginger
½ teaspoon Himalayan pink salt

1. Toss the pineapple slices with the sugar, cinnamon, ginger and salt. 2. Place the pineapple slices in a single layer on the dehydrator tray. Close and lock the air fryer lid. Select Dehydrate, set temperature to 120ºF (49ºC), and set time to 12 hours. Press Start.

Chewy Kiwi Chips

Prep time: 15 minutes | Cook time: 6 to 12 hours | Makes 10 to 12 slices

2 kiwis

1. Peel the kiwis, using a paring knife to slice the skin off or a vegetable peeler. 2. Slice the peeled kiwis into ¼-inch slices. 3. Place the kiwi slices on the dehydrator tray. Close and lock the air fryer lid. Select Dehydrate, set temperature to 135ºF (57ºC), and set time to 6 to 12 hours. Press Start. 4. These should be slightly chewy when done.

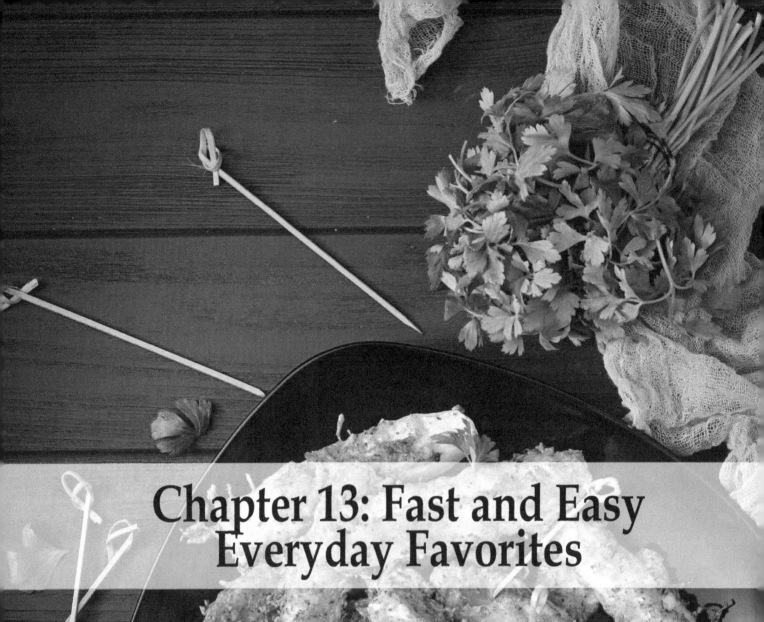

Chapter 13: Fast and Easy Everyday Favorites

Corn Fritters

Prep time: 15 minutes | Cook time: 8 minutes | Serves 6

1 cup self-rising flour

1 tablespoon sugar

1 teaspoon salt

1 large egg, lightly beaten

¼ cup buttermilk

¾ cup corn kernels

¼ cup minced onion

Cooking spray

1. Line the air fryer basket with parchment paper. 2. In a medium bowl, whisk the flour, sugar, and salt until blended. Stir in the egg and buttermilk. Add the corn and minced onion. Mix well. Shape the corn fritter batter into 12 balls. 3. Place the fritters on the parchment and spritz with oil. Close and lock the air fryer lid. Select Bake, set temperature to 350ºF (177ºC), and set time to 8 minutes. Press Start. Bake for 4 minutes. Flip the fritters, spritz them with oil, and bake for 4 minutes more until firm and lightly browned. 4. Serve immediately.

Baked Chorizo Scotch Eggs

Prep time: 5 minutes | Cook time: 15 to 20 minutes | Makes 4 eggs

1 pound (454 g) Mexican chorizo or other seasoned sausage meat

4 soft-boiled eggs plus 1 raw egg

1 tablespoon water

½ cup all-purpose flour

1 cup panko bread crumbs

Cooking spray

1. Divide the chorizo into 4 equal portions. Flatten each portion into a disc. Place a soft-boiled egg in the center of each disc. Wrap the chorizo around the egg, encasing it completely. Place the encased eggs on a plate and chill for at least 30 minutes. 2. Beat the raw egg with 1 tablespoon of water. Place the flour on a small plate and the panko on a second plate. Working with 1 egg at a time, roll the encased egg in the flour, then dip it in the egg mixture. Dredge the egg in the panko and place on a plate. Repeat with the remaining eggs. 3. Spray the eggs with oil and place in the air fryer basket. Close and lock the air fryer lid. Select Bake, set temperature to 360ºF (182ºC), and set time to 15 to 20 minutes. Press Start. Bake for 10 minutes. Turn and bake for an additional 5 to 10 minutes, or until browned and crisp on all sides. 4. Serve immediately.

Easy Cinnamon Toast

Prep time: 5 minutes | Cook time: 20 minutes | Serves 6

1½ teaspoons cinnamon

1½ teaspoons vanilla extract

½ cup sugar

2 teaspoons ground black pepper

2 tablespoons melted coconut oil

12 slices whole wheat bread

1. Combine all the ingredients, except for the bread, in a large bowl. Stir to mix well. 2. Dunk the bread in the bowl of mixture gently to coat and infuse well. Shake the excess off. 3. Arrange the bread slices in the air fryer basket. Close and lock the air fryer lid. Select Air Fry, set temperature to 400ºF (204ºC), and set time to 5 minutes. Press Start. Cook until golden brown. Flip the bread halfway through. You may need to cook in batches to avoid overcrowding. 4. Remove the bread slices from the basket and slice to serve.

Air Fried Broccoli

Prep time: 5 minutes | Cook time: 6 minutes | Serves 1

4 egg yolks
¼ cup butter, melted
2 cups coconut flour

Salt and pepper, to taste
2 cups broccoli florets

1. In a bowl, whisk the egg yolks and melted butter together. Throw in the coconut flour, salt and pepper, then stir again to combine well. 2. Dip each broccoli floret into the mixture and place in the air fryer basket. Close and lock the air fryer lid. Select Air Fry, set temperature to 400ºF (204ºC), and set time to 6 minutes. Press Start. Cook in batches if necessary. 3. Take care when removing them from the basket and serve immediately.

Simple Pea Delight

Prep time: 5 minutes | Cook time: 15 minutes | Serves 2 to 4

1 cup flour
1 teaspoon baking powder
3 eggs
1 cup coconut milk
1 cup cream cheese

3 tablespoons pea protein
½ cup chicken or turkey strips
Pinch of sea salt
1 cup mozzarella cheese

1. In a large bowl, mix all ingredients together using a large wooden spoon. 2. Spoon equal amounts of the mixture into muffin cups and place in air fryer basket. Close and lock the air fryer lid. Select Bake, set temperature to 390ºF (199ºC), and set time to 15 minutes. Press Start. 3. Serve immediately.

Bacon Pinwheels

Prep time: 10 minutes | Cook time: 10 minutes | Makes 8 pinwheels

1 sheet puff pastry
2 tablespoons maple syrup
¼ cup brown sugar

8 slices bacon
Ground black pepper, to taste
Cooking spray

1. Spritz the air fryer basket with cooking spray. 2. Roll the puff pastry into a 10-inch square with a rolling pin on a clean work surface, then cut the pastry into 8 strips. 3. Brush the strips with maple syrup and sprinkle with sugar, leaving a 1-inch far end uncovered. 4. Arrange each slice of bacon on each strip, leaving a ⅛-inch length of bacon hang over the end close to you. Sprinkle with black pepper. 5. From the end close to you, roll the strips into pinwheels, then dab the uncovered end with water and seal the rolls. 6. Arrange the pinwheels in the air fryer basket and spritz with cooking spray. Close and lock the air fryer lid. Select Air Fry, set temperature to 360ºF (182ºC), and set time to 10 minutes. Press Start. Cook until golden brown. Flip the pinwheels halfway through. 7. Serve immediately.

Cheesy Potato Patties

Prep time: 5 minutes | Cook time: 10 minutes | Serves 8

2 pounds (907 g) white potatoes
½ cup finely chopped scallions
½ teaspoon freshly ground black pepper, or more to taste
1 tablespoon fine sea salt
½ teaspoon hot paprika
2 cups shredded Colby cheese
¼ cup canola oil
1 cup crushed crackers

1. Boil the potatoes until soft. Dry them off and peel them before mashing thoroughly, leaving no lumps. 2. Combine the mashed potatoes with scallions, pepper, salt, paprika, and cheese. 3. Mold the mixture into balls with your hands and press with your palm to flatten them into patties. 4. In a shallow dish, combine the canola oil and crushed crackers. Coat the patties in the crumb mixture and place in air fryer basket. 5. Close and lock the air fryer lid. Select Bake, set temperature to 360ºF (182ºC), and set time to 10 minutes. Press Start. Bake the patties in multiple batches if necessary. 6. Serve hot.

Air Fried Shishito Peppers

Prep time: 5 minutes | Cook time: 5 minutes | Serves 4

½ pound (227 g) shishito peppers (about 24)
1 tablespoon olive oil
Coarse sea salt, to taste
Lemon wedges, for serving
Cooking spray

1. Spritz the air fryer basket with cooking spray. 2. Toss the peppers with olive oil in a large bowl to coat well. 3. Arrange the peppers in the air fryer basket. Close and lock the air fryer lid. Select Air Fry, set temperature to 400ºF (204ºC), and set time to 5 minutes. Press Start. Cook until blistered and lightly charred. Shake the basket and sprinkle the peppers with salt halfway through the cooking time. 4. Transfer the peppers onto a plate and squeeze the lemon wedges on top before serving.

Easy Roasted Asparagus

Prep time: 5 minutes | Cook time: 6 minutes | Serves 4

1 pound (454 g) asparagus, trimmed and halved crosswise
1 teaspoon extra-virgin olive oil
Salt and pepper, to taste
Lemon wedges, for serving

1. Toss the asparagus with the oil, ⅛ teaspoon salt, and ⅛ teaspoon pepper in bowl. Transfer to air fryer basket. 2. Close and lock the air fryer lid. Select Roast, set temperature to 400ºF (204ºC), and set time to 6 minutes. Press Start. Cook until tender and bright green, tossing halfway through cooking. 3. Season with salt and pepper and serve with lemon wedges.

Appendix 1: Measurement Conversion Chart

VOLUME EQUIVALENTS(DRY)

US STANDARD	METRIC (APPROXIMATE)
1/8 teaspoon	0.5 mL
1/4 teaspoon	1 mL
1/2 teaspoon	2 mL
3/4 teaspoon	4 mL
1 teaspoon	5 mL
1 tablespoon	15 mL
1/4 cup	59 mL
1/2 cup	118 mL
3/4 cup	177 mL
1 cup	235 mL
2 cups	475 mL
3 cups	700 mL
4 cups	1 L

VOLUME EQUIVALENTS(LIQUID)

US STANDARD	US STANDARD (OUNCES)	METRIC (APPROXIMATE)
2 tablespoons	1 fl.oz.	30 mL
1/4 cup	2 fl.oz.	60 mL
1/2 cup	4 fl.oz.	120 mL
1 cup	8 fl.oz.	240 mL
1 1/2 cup	12 fl.oz.	355 mL
2 cups or 1 pint	16 fl.oz.	475 mL
4 cups or 1 quart	32 fl.oz.	1 L
1 gallon	128 fl.oz.	4 L

WEIGHT EQUIVALENTS

US STANDARD	METRIC (APPROXIMATE)
1 ounce	28 g
2 ounces	57 g
5 ounces	142 g
10 ounces	284 g
15 ounces	425 g
16 ounces (1 pound)	455 g
1.5 pounds	680 g
2 pounds	907 g

TEMPERATURES EQUIVALENTS

FAHRENHEIT(F)	CELSIUS(C) (APPROXIMATE)
225 °F	107 °C
250 °F	120 °C
275 °F	135 °C
300 °F	150 °C
325 °F	160 °C
350 °F	180 °C
375 °F	190 °C
400 °F	205 °C
425 °F	220 °C
450 °F	235 °C
475 °F	245 °C
500 °F	260 °C

Appendix 2: Instant Pot Cooking Timetable

Dried Beans, Legumes and Lentils

Dried Beans and Legume	Dry (Minutes)	Soaked (Minutes)
Soy beans	25 – 30	20 – 25
Scarlet runner	20 – 25	10 – 15
Pinto beans	25 – 30	20 – 25
Peas	15 – 20	10 – 15
Navy beans	25 – 30	20 – 25
Lima beans	20 – 25	10 – 15
Lentils, split, yellow (moong dal)	15 – 18	N/A
Lentils, split, red	15 – 18	N/A
Lentils, mini, green (brown)	15 – 20	N/A
Lentils, French green	15 – 20	N/A
Kidney white beans	35 – 40	20 – 25
Kidney red beans	25 – 30	20 – 25
Great Northern beans	25 – 30	20 – 25
Pigeon peas	20 – 25	15 – 20
Chickpeas (garbanzo bean chickpeas)	35 – 40	20 – 25
Cannellini beans	35 – 40	20 – 25
Black-eyed peas	20 – 25	10 – 15
Black beans	20 – 25	10 – 15

Fish and Seafood

Fish and Seafood	Fresh (minutes)	Frozen (minutes)
Shrimp or Prawn	1 to 2	2 to 3
Seafood soup or stock	6 to 7	7 to 9
Mussels	2 to 3	4 to 6
Lobster	3 to 4	4 to 6
Fish, whole (snapper, trout, etc.)	5 to 6	7 to 10
Fish steak	3 to 4	4 to 6
Fish fillet,	2 to 3	3 to 4
Crab	3 to 4	5 to 6

Fruits

Fruits	Fresh (in Minutes)	Dried (in Minutes)
Raisins	N/A	4 to 5
Prunes	2 to 3	4 to 5
Pears, whole	3 to 4	4 to 6
Pears, slices or halves	2 to 3	4 to 5
Peaches	2 to 3	4 to 5
Apricots, whole or halves	2 to 3	3 to 4
Apples, whole	3 to 4	4 to 6
Apples, in slices or pieces	2 to 3	3 to 4

Meat

Meat and Cuts	Cooking Time (minutes)	Meat and Cuts	Cooking Time (minutes)
Veal, roast	35 to 45	Duck, with bones, cut up	10 to 12
Veal, chops	5 to 8	Cornish Hen, whole	10 to 15
Turkey, drumsticks (leg)	15 to 20	Chicken, whole	20 to 25
Turkey, breast, whole, with bones	25 to 30	Chicken, legs, drumsticks, or thighs	10 to 15
Turkey, breast, boneless	15 to 20	Chicken, with bones, cut up	10 to 15
Quail, whole	8 to 10	Chicken, breasts	8 to 10
Pork, ribs	20 to 25	Beef, stew	15 to 20
Pork, loin roast	55 to 60	Beef, shanks	25 to 30
Pork, butt roast	45 to 50	Beef, ribs	25 to 30
Pheasant	20 to 25	Beef, steak, pot roast, round, rump, brisket or blade, small chunks, chuck,	25 to 30
Lamb, stew meat	10 to 15		
Lamb, leg	35 to 45	Beef, pot roast, steak, rump, round, chuck, blade or brisket, large	35 to 40
Lamb, cubes,	10 t0 15		
Ham slice	9 to 12	Beef, ox-tail	40 to 50
Ham picnic shoulder	25 to 30	Beef, meatball	10 to 15
Duck, whole	25 to 30	Beef, dressed	20 to 25

Appendix 3: Instant Pot Cooking Timetable

Vegetables (fresh/frozen)

Vegetable	Fresh (minutes)	Frozen (minutes)	Vegetable	Fresh (minutes)	Frozen (minutes)
Zucchini, slices or chunks	2 to 3	3 to 4	Mixed vegetables	2 to 3	3 to 4
Yam, whole, small	10 to 12	12 to 14	Leeks	2 to 4	3 to 5
Yam, whole, large	12 to 15	15 to 19	Greens (collards, beet greens, spinach, kale, turnip greens, swiss chard) chopped	3 to 6	4 to 7
Yam, in cubes	7 to 9	9 to 11			
Turnip, chunks	2 to 4	4 to 6	Green beans, whole	2 to 3	3 to 4
Tomatoes, whole	3 to 5	5 to 7	Escarole, chopped	1 to 2	2 to 3
Tomatoes, in quarters	2 to 3	4 to 5	Endive	1 to 2	2 to 3
Sweet potato, whole, small	10 to 12	12 to 14	Eggplant, chunks or slices	2 to 3	3 to 4
Sweet potato, whole, large	12 to 15	15 to 19	Corn, on the cob	3 to 4	4 to 5
Sweet potato, in cubes	7 to 9	9 to 11	Corn, kernels	1 to 2	2 to 3
Sweet pepper, slices or chunks	1 to 3	2 to 4	Collard	4 to 5	5 to 6
Squash, butternut, slices or chunks	8 to 10	10 to 12	Celery, chunks	2 to 3	3 to 4
Squash, acorn, slices or chunks	6 to 7	8 to 9	Cauliflower flowerets	2 to 3	3 to 4
Spinach	1 to 2	3 to 4	Carrots, whole or chunked	2 to 3	3 to 4
Rutabaga, slices	3 to 5	4 to 6	Carrots, sliced or shredded	1 to 2	2 to 3
Rutabaga, chunks	4 to 6	6 to 8	Cabbage, red, purple or green, wedges	3 to 4	4 to 5
Pumpkin, small slices or chunks	4 to 5	6 to 7	Cabbage, red, purple or green, shredded	2 to 3	3 to 4
Pumpkin, large slices or chunks	8 to 10	10 to 14	Brussel sprouts, whole	3 to 4	4 to 5
Potatoes, whole, large	12 to 15	15 to 19	Broccoli, stalks	3 to 4	4 to 5
Potatoes, whole, baby	10 to 12	12 to 14	Broccoli, flowerets	2 to 3	3 to 4
Potatoes, in cubes	7 to 9	9 to 11	Beets, small roots, whole	11 to 13	13 to 15
Peas, in the pod	1 to 2	2 to 3	Beets, large roots, whole	20 to 25	25 to 30
Peas, green	1 to 2	2 to 3	Beans, green/yellow or wax, whole, trim ends and strings	1 to 2	2 to 3
Parsnips, sliced	1 to 2	2 to 3			
Parsnips, chunks	2 to 4	4 to 6	Asparagus, whole or cut	1 to 2	2 to 3
Onions, sliced	2 to 3	3 to 4	Artichoke, whole, trimmed without leaves	9 to 11	11 to 13
Okra	2 to 3	3 to 4	Artichoke, hearts	4 to 5	5 to 6

Rice and Grains

Rice & Grain	Water Quantity (Grain: Water ratios)	Cooking Time (in Minutes)	Rice & Grain	Water Quantity (Grain: Water ratios)	Cooking Time (in Minutes)
Wheat berries	1:3	25 to 30	Oats, steel-cut	1:1	10
Spelt berries	1:3	15 to 20	Oats, quick cooking	1:1	6
Sorghum	1:3	20 to 25	Millet	1:1	10 to 12
Rice, wild	1:3	25 to 30	Kamut, whole	1:3	10 to 12
Rice, white	1:1.5	8	Couscous	1:2	5 to 8
Rice, Jasmine	1:1	4 to 10	Corn, dried, half	1:3	25 to 30
Rice, Brown	1:1.3	22 to 28	Congee, thin	1:6 ~ 1:7	15 to 20
Rice, Basmati	1:1.5	4 to 8	Congee, thick	1:4 ~ 1:5	15 to 20
Quinoa, quick cooking	1:2	8	Barley, pot	1:3 ~ 1:4	25 to 30
Porridge, thin	1:6 ~ 1:7	15 to 20	Barley, pearl	1:4	25 to 30

Appendix 4 : Air Fryer Cooking Chart

Beef

Item	Temp (°F)	Time (mins)	Item	Temp (°F)	Time (mins)
Beef Eye Round Roast (4 lbs.)	400 °F	45 to 55	Meatballs (1-inch)	370 °F	7
Burger Patty (4 oz.)	370 °F	16 to 20	Meatballs (3-inch)	380 °F	10
Filet Mignon (8 oz.)	400 °F	18	Ribeye, bone-in (1-inch, 8 oz)	400 °F	10 to 15
Flank Steak (1.5 lbs.)	400 °F	12	Sirloin steaks (1-inch, 12 oz)	400 °F	9 to 14
Flank Steak (2 lbs.)	400 °F	20 to 28			

Chicken

Item	Temp (°F)	Time (mins)	Item	Temp (°F)	Time (mins)
Breasts, bone in (1 ¼ lb.)	370 °F	25	Legs, bone-in (1 ¾ lb.)	380 °F	30
Breasts, boneless (4 oz)	380 °F	12	Thighs, boneless (1 ½ lb.)	380 °F	18 to 20
Drumsticks (2 ½ lb.)	370 °F	20	Wings (2 lb.)	400 °F	12
Game Hen (halved 2 lb.)	390 °F	20	Whole Chicken	360 °F	75
Thighs, bone-in (2 lb.)	380 °F	22	Tenders	360 °F	8 to 10

Pork & Lamb

Item	Temp (°F)	Time (mins)	Item	Temp (°F)	Time (mins)
Bacon (regular)	400 °F	5 to 7	Pork Tenderloin	370 °F	15
Bacon (thick cut)	400 °F	6 to 10	Sausages	380 °F	15
Pork Loin (2 lb.)	360 °F	55	Lamb Loin Chops (1-inch thick)	400 °F	8 to 12
Pork Chops, bone in (1-inch, 6.5 oz)	400 °F	12	Rack of Lamb (1.5 – 2 lb.)	380 °F	22

Fish & Seafood

Item	Temp (°F)	Time (mins)	Item	Temp (°F)	Time (mins)
Calamari (8 oz)	400 °F	4	Tuna Steak	400 °F	7 to 10
Fish Fillet (1-inch, 8 oz)	400 °F	10	Scallops	400 °F	5 to 7
Salmon, fillet (6 oz)	380 °F	12	Shrimp	400 °F	5
Swordfish steak	400 °F	10			

Appendix 5 : Air Fryer Cooking Chart

Vegetables					
INGREDIENT	AMOUNT	PREPARATION	OIL	TEMP	COOK TIME
Asparagus	2 bunches	Cut in half, trim stems	2 Tbsp	420°F	12-15 mins
Beets	1½ lbs	Peel, cut in ½-inch cubes	1Tbsp	390°F	28-30 mins
Bell peppers (for roasting)	4 peppers	Cut in quarters, remove seeds	1Tbsp	400°F	15-20 mins
Broccoli	1 large head	Cut in 1-2-inch florets	1Tbsp	400°F	15-20 mins
Brussels sprouts	1lb	Cut in half, remove stems	1Tbsp	425°F	15-20 mins
Carrots	1lb	Peel, cut in ¼-inch rounds	1 Tbsp	425°F	10-15 mins
Cauliflower	1 head	Cut in 1-2-inch florets	2 Tbsp	400°F	20-22 mins
Corn on the cob	7 ears	Whole ears, remove husks	1 Tbps	400°F	14-17 mins
Green beans	1 bag (12 oz)	Trim	1 Tbps	420°F	18-20 mins
Kale (for chips)	4 oz	Tear into pieces,remove stems	None	325°F	5-8 mins
Mushrooms	16 oz	Rinse, slice thinly	1 Tbps	390°F	25-30 mins
Potatoes, russet	1½ lbs	Cut in 1-inch wedges	1 Tbps	390°F	25-30 mins
Potatoes, russet	1lb	Hand-cut fries, soak 30 mins in cold water, then pat dry	½ -3 Tbps	400°F	25-28 mins
Potatoes, sweet	1lb	Hand-cut fries, soak 30 mins in cold water, then pat dry	1 Tbps	400°F	25-28 mins
Zucchini	1lb	Cut in eighths lengthwise, then cut in half	1 Tbps	400°F	15-20 mins

Made in the USA
Monee, IL
29 September 2023

43694167R00063